Contents

Acknowledgements

Many people have contributed to this book, some knowingly. I have learned a great deal from all the researchers with whom I have worked over the years, particularly my former colleagues at the Policy Studies Institute in London. The book has also been greatly improved as a result of the various comments made by reviewers of previous editions. I would like to single out Kerrie Burgess of the State Library of New South Wales, who provided a thorough and constructive critique of the third edition. Finally, I owe a very great deal to Elaine Kempson who has taught me so much over the years.

Introduction
Types of research

There are many different types of research. This book is about social research – about research into people and institutions and the relationships between them.

People have different motives for undertaking research. Some do it for academic reasons – as part of a course of study or to advance our *theoretical* understanding of the world around us. Others do it in an attempt to solve a problem or to develop a *practical* understanding of a situation. They may use the same research methods and manage their work in similar ways, but their starting points will be different. Their motivations will affect the design of the research and will, to a great extent, determine the way the results are interpreted and reported.

Academic research

Academic research is primarily concerned with developing a theoretical explanation or understanding of an issue. For most people the motivation will be clear – the research will be undertaken as a step towards the acquisition of an academic or professional qualification. For some, it will be an essential part of an academic job. In both cases the primary motivation should be reinforced by a more general desire to increase the sum of knowledge and understanding or, at least, to reduce levels of uncertainty.

Undergraduate and masters' degrees

The first step on the academic research ladder will usually be a dissertation completed as part of a first or master's degree. This kind of research is intended to demonstrate the researcher's grasp of the subject or discipline and to provide a basic level of training and practice in systematic investigation. It also demonstrates the researcher's ability to handle and manage information and data, to organize their time and to communicate something sensible through 10 or 20,000 words of continuous prose.

The research is usually very self-contained and relatively modest in scale. It begins with a review of what others have written on the subject, followed by the definition of the research question that the dissertation seeks to explore. This question is then explored through a small-scale piece of research, perhaps involving the collection and analysis of some data or occasionally a detailed analytical review of the literature. Here the aim is not really to produce definitive answers, rather it is to demonstrate that the candidate can handle research methods, and data, satisfactorily.

The results are brought together into a conclusion that addresses the research question and that, ideally, relates the findings to the theoretical or conceptual framework established by others. The study is then written up, handsomely bound and read by the researcher, the supervisor, the examiner and the researcher's mum. And that is about it.

Doctorates

The next step is the PhD. Here practice varies from country to country – in Britain PhD degrees are usually wholly based on the candidate's research, while in other countries students also have to complete course-work. In some instances, candidates first undertake work for an MPhil, usually registering with an option to extend the research for a PhD if progress is satisfactory. Whatever the local practice, however, the essence of the exercise is the conduct of a substantial piece of research. If research for a master's degree is part of the researcher's training, the PhD is their chance to demonstrate their research skills.

The PhD researcher working in the social sciences will be expected to build on the work of others. They should draw on a range of different theoretical perspectives to arrive at a research proposition or an hypothesis which can then be tested through research. This usually means some form of empirical study, collecting data which can be analysed to shed light on the issue in question. It is, therefore, critically important to frame the research question or hypothesis in such a way that it can be tested through empirical research.

The research itself will be a major undertaking, perhaps involving a range of different research methods and lasting a year or more. The candidate will be expected to break new ground, develop new techniques or to explore previously uncharted territory.

The level of analysis is, therefore, critical and should lead to conclusions that prove or disprove the validity of the hypothesis, that advance new theoretical explanations or that throw new light on the basic research proposition.

The results of the whole process will be presented in a thesis which will extend to many pages. It will set out the conceptual framework within which the research has been formulated; it will present the results, usually in great detail; these will be followed by the analysis and from this will flow the conclusions. The whole thing will be handsomely bound and read by the researcher, the supervisor and the examiners.

Career academics

For some, the PhD leads on to a career as an academic and an expectation that they will continue to carry out research. Hereafter the emphasis shifts again. There are no examiners to be satisfied. Instead academic researchers have to meet the often stringent expectations of their peers. Their proposals will need to satisfy a number of referees before they are given the money they need to carry out research. Then, at the end of the process, results will be subject to a similar process of peer review.

The distinguishing characteristic of academic research at this level is the concern with concepts and theories. The initial research proposition will be grounded in a theoretical or conceptual context which, in most cases, has been established through prior research. The research itself should then add something to this body of theory. It may introduce a completely new theoretical perspective. It may qualify one that has already been advanced. It may even set out to demolish or disprove a theory.

The research may lead to a report, even a published monograph. But the main means of disseminating the results will be through articles in refereed journals or papers presented at conferences.

We can say, therefore, that academic research is more concerned with developing a theoretical explanation of why a problem is a problem than it is with finding a solution to the problem.

Applied and policy research

In contrast to academic research, applied research is characterized by its concern with problems and their solution. There is also a whole body of social research that is simply concerned with monitoring developments in the world around us and so increasing our understanding of what is going on. The regular social surveys conducted by governments fall into this category, as does much of the research commissioned by organizations to monitor the effects of their policies. A good deal of applied research is undertaken by researchers employed by the organizations that they study.

The defining characteristic of applied research is the fact that someone is likely to take action of some kind based on the results of the research. It is, therefore, critically important to be clear from the outset about the nature of the problem that is to be addressed and also to have a thorough understanding of the needs and expectations of the people who may be called upon to act on the results.

Organizations

A great deal of applied research takes place within organizations as they try to overcome problems and improve their efficiency and effectiveness. The work is undertaken by members of the organization's staff and it can range from small-scale investigations into minor problems, up to large projects tackling strategic issues. There is usually little dispute about the nature and scope of the problem and there is a reasonable expectation that those undertaking the research will be aware of the requirements of those who will take action based on the results.

In many cases, however, organizations choose to use people from outside the organization to carry out the research. Management and other, more specialist, consultancies spend much of their time undertaking this kind of applied research. They are brought in to investigate a problem, to identify a solution and to recommend a strategy for the organization.

Such consultants or researchers always have to overcome their lack of familiarity with the organization. They will usually expect to spend some time working with those most directly concerned to define the scope and nature of the problem. They will also need to understand the organizational context sufficiently so that they can make recommendations that are likely to be workable.

Social policy

There is also a growing body of applied research that deals with more general social problems. The growing number of policy-related or applied research institutes undertake work of this kind for government departments and other public sector bodies or for research foundations. Many of these institutes are independent. Some, particularly in Japan, are attached to, or sponsored by, large corporations. Many others have developed within the university sector where they carry out applied research that is quite distinct from, although no less rigorous than the more conventional academic research.

These specialist applied research institutes adopt a slightly different approach to research questions. They do not just try to find an answer to a particular question, they try to put the question into a broader, more strategic context. To this extent they attempt to find out why a problem is a problem before going on to solve it.

Clearly, theory has some part to play in this kind of applied, or strategic, research. Theories are an attempt to explain how the world works and how the different parts interact with each other. Any attempt to develop a strategic approach to applied research will need to look beyond the immediate problem and look for underlying causes or explanations and for this, theories are of obvious value as explanations of why the problem is a problem. But the need to provide practical solutions means that strategic research tends to place more reliance on empirical data and evidence than it does on theories and concepts.

A continuum

While, at the extremes, there are very clear differences between academic and applied research, the extremes represent the end-points on a continuum. At one extreme we have academics who are solely concerned with building theories and constructing conceptual frameworks to explain social phenomena. At the other we have consultants and research workers within organizations attempting to find solutions to pressing problems. In between we have strategic or applied social researchers, many of them working within research institutes, who are trying to monitor what is going on in the world or to identify the underlying causes of social problems so that they can recommend generally applicable and long-lasting solutions.

Approaches to research

Cutting across the distinction between academic and applied research, it is possible to identify a number of different approaches to the design of social research. It is not simply a question of which methods are used – the same method can be used in a number of different approaches. Rather, the approach reflects the nature of the subject or issue to be studied.

Survey research

This is the most common form of social research. The researcher begins with a question, or the need to discover something. They design a survey to collect the necessary data. They then process and analyse it, interpret the results and come to a set of conclusions. It is a basic approach that can be used to find out about a wide range of behaviour, attitudes and opinions.

Social surveys are predominantly concerned with asking people questions and analysing their answers. Beneath that apparent simplicity, however, lies a sophisticated set of methods designed to elicit responses efficiently and accurately. The second part of this book deals with techniques for conducting surveys and analysing the results.

Surveys are the common denominator of other approaches to research. They can be used in a range of different circumstances and for different purposes. They are the basic tools with which social researchers should be familiar.

Experimental research

This approach to research is largely derived from scientific research method. The essence is an attempt to conduct a test and to observe the results. The difference between experimental research in the pure sciences and experimental research in social science lies in the fact that in the former, research can be carried out in a laboratory where it is relatively easy to control the environment. In contrast, social science research is largely carried out in the real world where the environment is changing and unpredictable and where it is very difficult to control the variables.

To overcome some of these difficulties, experimental social science uses control groups to compare what happens to one group that is subjected to the test with the behaviour, attitudes or opinions of another group that is not. Clearly, much depends on the initial similarity of the groups and the extent to which it is possible to ensure that, during the course of the experiment, they remain broadly similar.

To add validity to the results of an experiment, it is normal in the scientific community to replicate the research to ensure that the results are not the product of random chance. Such replication is uncommon in the social science community.

Action research

Action research involves integrating research into a process of social development to monitor what happens and to evaluate the outcomes. In some cases, the whole activity is envisaged as a research project, in others the research is grafted on in an attempt to measure the effects of the activity.

Many of the problems with action research stem from the difficulty of disentangling cause from effect. The very fact that the research is taking place distorts the activity and creates an unreal situation. The action researcher must, therefore, achieve a difficult balance between participating in the activity and remaining sufficiently separate to be able to offer objective judgments.

In theory the researcher observes what is taking place, collecting data as the activity progresses and analysing it to identify the effects. At the end of the process, they produce a report that evaluates what has been achieved and sets out the lessons that can be learned. This is known in the trade as summative evaluation. In practice things are more complicated. The researcher is often called upon to offer a judgment while the activity is in progress – and it is hard to avoid the temptation to contribute ideas and conclusions that might ultimately increase the success of the activity. Formally this is known as formative evaluation.

It is also important to resist the temptation to do what is known in the trade as 'going native'. This is shorthand for what happens when a researcher begins to identify with the service or activity that they are researching and they lose the objectivity that should be an essential component of all social research. The closer one gets to the subjects of the research, the more difficult it is to maintain the necessary degree of isolation.

Case studies

Case studies are used when it is necessary to develop a detailed understanding of what is happening in complex circumstances. Often a large-scale survey will not provide the depth of understanding required. It then becomes necessary to look in detail at what is happening in a smaller number of instances or cases. This provides greater depth at the expense of breadth.

Clearly, the choice of case studies is critical. They should be selected so that they broadly represent the total population being surveyed. They will never be representative in a statistical sense. Rather, they should reflect the main characteristics of the whole population.

When conducting case study research, it is always important to establish clearly the context within which the case studies operate. Case studies of local authorities should, for example, reflect the main types of local authority unit in terms of the size of the population served, the rural-urban split, perhaps the political complexion of the council, and so on. The research should codify this context so that the results can be interpreted correctly.

Evaluation and performance measurement

Much social research is concerned with evaluating the progress of a service or the impact of a policy, or with measuring the performance of a service. With this research it is important to make a clear distinction between efficiency, effectiveness and impact.

Efficiency is the measure of the ratio between inputs and outputs. It attempts to assess whether a given level of output can be achieved with more or fewer inputs. Or whether, given a fixed level of inputs, the level of output can be increased or decreased.

Effectiveness is concerned with the extent to which a service achieves its objectives. Here, clearly, it is important to know what the service objectives are at the outset, and to be able to express them in measurable terms. Effectiveness cannot be divorced from efficiency – few effective services are inefficient, while many efficient services can be shown to be ineffective.

Impact is something different again. It is concerned with the effect that a service has on those that receive it. It is very difficult to measure, largely because, in the social sphere, it is extremely difficult to separate cause from effect – consider how difficult it is, for example, to measure the impact of an advertising campaign.

So, when asked to evaluate a service or to measure performance, it is important to establish whether you are being asked to measure efficiency, effectiveness or impact.

Evaluation and performance measurement also involve a significant degree of comparison – comparing the service provided now with what has gone before, or comparing the outcomes of this service with another which is delivered in a different way. Here it is really important to be certain that you are comparing like with like. Or if you are not, then to be clear about what the underlying differences are.

SUMMARY

There are many different types of research ranging from pure academic research at one extreme to applied and policy-related research at the other.

Academic research is mainly concerned with the development of a theoretical understanding of an issue. Applied research is concerned with understanding the nature and causes of problems so that they may be solved and with monitoring the development of the world around us.

There are also many different approaches to the design of social research projects:

- Survey research is the most common approach. Surveys are also the common denominator of social research – they are a technique that can be deployed in a number of other approaches.
- Experimental research has been derived from the traditional scientific research model and involves measuring the effect of something on a particular group and then comparing it with an independent control group.

- Action research involves integrating research into a process of social development to monitor what happens and to evaluate the outcomes.
- Case studies are used to provide a detailed understanding of what is happening in complex circumstances.
- Evaluation and performance measurement require a clear understanding of the differences between efficiency, effectiveness and impact. There is also an implicit notion of comparison – over time or between different services or activities. It is, therefore, important to be clear that one is comparing like with like.

Part 1
The research process

1

Develop the research objectives

The importance of research aims and objectives cannot be over-stressed. It is vital to have a very clear understanding of what the research is about and what you are actually trying to achieve. You need to know this. And you need to be able to communicate it to others.

Carrying out a research project is rather like going on a journey. It is a linear process during which, in theory at least, you move from your starting point to your objective and then tell others the story of your journey. In practice it can become much more complex.

Once begun, there are few opportunities to retrace your steps if you get lost or side-tracked. The project develops a momentum of its own and it is often difficult to slow things down or to alter course. There are also lots of fascinating by-ways and side routes that might be interesting to explore. This is made worse by the fact that as the research – or the journey – progresses, the level of complexity increases and it is easy to find yourself in the middle of a metaphorical forest with many paths leading in different directions and no clear indication of which is the best one to take.

Assuming that you manage to find your way through all this, you still need to retain a clear idea about where you are going so that you know when you have reached your destination.

A clear, unambiguous research aim coupled with a precise statement of research objectives will provide you with an initial sense of direction. It will enable you to design the research project, selecting the most appropriate methods. It will also provide the basis for managing the research once the project is underway. It will also be an invaluable guide when it comes to analysing the results and making sense of it all.

A clear idea of what you are going to do is also an essential part of obtaining support from others, whether they be stakeholders, potential funders or subjects of the research.

Defining the research issue

The starting point is the definition of the research issue or problem. What is it that you are trying to discover through the research? This is an easy question to ask but a difficult one to answer.

Many people find it difficult to get their minds around what it is that they are studying through the research. This is particularly true for students trying to settle on a topic for a dissertation. Some begin with a clear concern about an issue. Many others start from a general interest in a topic and then need to refine and shape their interest into something researchable.

Applied researchers have things a little easier. In-house researchers are usually asked to conduct research into a specific topic or issue, although, in many cases, they may be the one to suggest the research. Other professional researchers are given an extensive brief or specification which describes what the commissioning body expects to achieve from the research. Even here, though, it is necessary to think through exactly what the research issue is.

The thing to look for is the essential element of the project – the one thing that characterizes it or distinguishes it from all other work and that encompasses the essential thrust of the research. One way to do this is to ask some basic questions:

- What are you trying to achieve?
- What are the important issues?
- Who will benefit from, or be affected by the project?
- What things will change as a result of the project?
- Why has the project been established?

Let us suppose that you begin with an interest in organizational change and the long-term effects of training, or have been asked to look at the impact of the organization's training programme. The answers to the questions might run like this.

What are you trying to achieve?

The research is trying to discover whether or not training programmes bring about lasting changes in attitudes and behaviour among staff and, in particular, whether training increases staff motivation and makes them more receptive to organizational change.

What are the important issues?

Some of the important issues are associated with attitudes: the assumption that attitudes can lead to resistance to change, the nature of attitudes themselves and their durability, the extent to which training can change attitudes, and the relationship between attitudes and behaviour.

Another issue is concerned with motivation: there is an assumption that training improves motivation – is this valid? There are other issues concerned with the training itself: what kind of training is envisaged, who will receive it and how will it be delivered, do different styles of training produce different results, who controls the training, and over what period will the training take place?

Finally, there is a set of issues concerned with measurement: how do we measure changes in attitudes, behaviour and motivation?

Who will benefit from, or be affected by the project?

The main beneficiaries of the research will be the managers of the organization. Clearly the staff receiving the training will be directly affected. It might also be necessary to take their colleagues into consideration. And possibly their immediate managers might need to be included in the research. In the case of public services, it might be necessary to take the views of service users into account. In addition to all of these immediate stakeholders, there will be others who have an interest in the results of the research. These other interested parties could include: managers of other organizations, academics, students and trade unionists.

What things will change as a result of the project?

There is an assumption that attitudes, behaviour and motivation will change as a result of the training, but how will these changes be measured? How will the research take account of any changes in the pattern of training itself? How, indeed, will the researcher take account of other changes that might be taking place within the organization during the process of the research?

Why has the project been established?

This can be critical. If you are a student developing the research project as a piece of work to be completed as part of an academic course, we might expect a fairly small-scale project which sets out to demonstrate the successful use of research methods. If, on the other hand, you are a researcher employed by a large corporation which is concerned about the cost-effectiveness of its training budget, the project is likely to be rather different in both scale and nature.

At this stage in the process, you, as the intending researcher, are usually rather too well aware of the complexities that you are being called upon to study. But you are beginning to develop the basic understanding that is necessary for the work. The next step is to refine things until you are left with the essence of the issue – and a project that is within your capabilities and resources.

Again, you can proceed by asking a series of questions:

- Despite all the complexity, what is it that you are really interested in?
- Are there any issues that can be left to another occasion?
- Are there things that are simply not capable of measurement?

It might be, for example, that you decide that the essence of the issue is the relationship between training, attitudes and resistance to change. You might conclude that the question of motivation is one that, given the resources at your disposal, is outside the scope of the project. And from your reading around the subject, you may decide that measuring the association between attitudes and behaviour is simply too complex an issue to be covered by this particular project.

Articulating the research aim

You are now getting to the point where you can begin to express the precise aim of the research. You should try to encompass things in one single, clear, unambiguous sentence. This should describe the essence of the study; it should omit nothing and include everything.

In our example, the first draft of the aim might be:

> The aim of the research is to test whether or not the training provided in the organization brings about lasting changes in staff attitudes and reduces resistance to change.

Be warned, though, it is seldom possible to get the aim right first time. Look at the aim expressed above. It assumes a causal chain: training leads to changes in attitudes which in turn reduces resistance to change. But by now you have realized that what you are really interested in is whether or not training can reduce resistance to change. You have been assuming that it is first necessary to change attitudes but this is not necessarily the case – higher levels of skill may increase staff confidence and make the introduction of change easier, even though their attitudes remain fixed.

So, it is probably worth changing the aim around and emphasizing just the two elements of training and resistance to change:

> The aim of the research is to test whether or not training can reduce resistance to change among staff.

This statement is clear, unambiguous and expressed in a single sentence.

It is worth working away at your research aim until you can also express it in this way. If you find yourself with sub-clauses, or more than one sentence, it may well be that you have more than one piece of research in mind or that you are building in too much complexity from the outset.

If all else fails, imagine that you are walking down the corridor and the person in charge of the organization is walking towards you. 'What are you doing over the next few weeks?' they ask. You have to respond with something clear and simple as they walk by. What would you say?

I have, perhaps, laboured the point a little, but not without good reason. Good research depends on having a clear aim from the outset. Everyone associated with the research should share an unambiguous understanding of what it is all about. And you need to start with something simple because things get much more complex later on.

Specifying the objectives

Having articulated the overall aim of the project, the next step is to specify the objectives that will have to be achieved in order to reach or satisfy the ultimate aim of the research. Put simply, the objectives define the things that have to be done during the research.

Some projects naturally break down into a number of discrete elements. In other cases it is more difficult to identify the component parts. One way to overcome this is to think through a chronological sequence: what has to be done first, what will come second, and so on.

In the case of the project on training and organizational change, the research could be approached in one of two ways. You could either do a before-and-after study, measuring resistance to change before the organization embarked on a training programme and comparing the results with the position after the training. Or you could compare resistance to change in organizations with big training programmes with that in those that provided little training for their staff.

Let us assume that you decide on the former approach – the before-and-after study – and that you had been asked by a particular organization that was planning to expand its training programme.

The first thing that you would have to do is to develop an instrument to measure the extent of resistance to change. To do this, you would probably need to draw on other research into organizational change, developing and adapting research instruments that had been used by others. So, the first two objectives might look like this:

- To undertake a review of research into resistance to change within organizations.
- From this review, to develop instruments to measure the extent of resistance to change among staff within the organization.

The third objective would naturally follow:

- To measure resistance to change among the staff before the training programme is launched.

You would need to monitor the training programme, noting which groups of staff were trained, whether some received more training than others and, perhaps, assessing the reactions to the training events as they took place. You would then be in a position to repeat the measurement in order to assess the extent to which resistance had shifted. The fourth and fifth objectives then become:

- To monitor the progress of the training programme.
- At the end of the programme, to assess whether or not there has been any alteration in the level of resistance to change among staff.

You could go on to add a final objective, stating that you will analyse the results and produce a report containing recommendations for action. But this can often be assumed.

Expressing specific objectives in this way forces you, from the outset, to think through how you will approach the research. It provides a framework for the selection of the most appropriate methods and, critically, it enables you to begin the task of planning and costing the work.

Clear objectives also help funders, research workers and the subjects of research to understand what is going on and to appreciate how each component fits into the whole picture.

The research project should now be taking shape and it becomes possible to think about the methods to be used, the time and resources that will be required and the likely problems and critical points that will arise.

From here on, things should start to get easier.

SUMMARY

It is essential to have a clear understanding of the research project's aim and objectives.

The starting point is the definition of the research issue. This can be clarified by asking a series of questions:

* What are you trying to achieve?
* What are the important issues?
* Who will benefit from, or be affected by the project?
* What things will change as a result of the project?

It is usually necessary to refine things further by asking:

* Despite all the complexity, what is it that you are really interested in?
* Are there any issues that can be left to another occasion?
* Are there things that are simply not capable of measurement?

It should then be possible to articulate the research aim. This should describe the essence of the project in a single clear, unambiguous sentence. The next step is to specify the objectives. These define the things that have to be done during the research.

2
Design and plan the study

The overall shape of the project will be determined to a large extent by the aim and objectives. In the example of research into training and organizational change, a decision had to be made early on about whether to use a before-and-after approach or one that relied on comparisons between organizations. And so it is with most projects. Even though the overall shape may be fixed by factors outside your control, there is still much to be done to design and plan the study in detail.

Resource constraints

First it is necessary to be aware of the constraints on the resources available to you. Essentially you need to think about money, time and expertise. Each is equally important.

Money

The overall amount of money available will play a large part in determining the design of the research. If you are being contracted by an organization to carry out work on their behalf, you clearly have to work within the budget they set. Research is a labour-intensive process and so most of this budget will be taken up by staff costs. Basically, the amount of money available dictates the number of days that can be spent on the project and thus determines its overall size.

If the research is part of your job within an organization there is usually a less stringent financial constraint. Most of the staff costs are likely to be covered, unless it is necessary to employ additional researchers, and the budget will be used for incidental expenses like the costs of conducting a survey. However, financial resources are never unlimited and before settling on the design you should check that money is available to spend on the research.

At the other end of the scale, if you are a student, it will probably be a case of considering whether or not you can afford the postage, copying and stationery costs associated with undertaking a postal survey.

Time

Here you need to think about two different sorts of time: elapsed time and research days. Elapsed time is simply the time between the start and finish of a project. For a student, the deadline is the submission date for the dissertation. On a research contract there will almost certainly be an equally severe cut-off point. In-house researchers may have their deadline set by something like the date of a board meeting. The elapsed time will determine the overall size and shape of a project.

More critical, though, is the number of research days that can be spent on the work. If the elapsed time for a project is three months and there are two research workers, there are, in theory about 180 research days available to the designer of the project. In practice, there is clearly much less than that. People need time off at weekends, they need holidays and they occasionally get taken sick. They also spend time in training, meetings and in a wide range of administrative tasks. In reality, few people can work more than 200 productive days each year. So two people working full-time for three months are likely to be able to do 100 days work.

Expertise

The expertise available is an important constraint on the design of research projects. While it is always nice to be able to extend your range of research skills, it is a foolish research designer who attempts a project that is outside their present range of expertise.

There are, of course, a number of ways in which it is possible to compensate for limited research skills. You could recruit a research worker who has the skills, although this is a risky business – the likelihood of finding someone with the right set of skills who is available at the right time is small. You could buy them in by using consultants or research companies for specialist tasks: it is common practice, for example, to sub-contract large surveys to market research companies. Another option might be to recruit an advisory committee made up of researchers who could advise on technical aspects of the work. But it is best to ground the project in the skills and expertise readily available to you.

Efficiency and economy in design

Once you know what resources you have to work with you can begin to design the project. This is where complexity can begin to creep in. Try hard to keep things simple – it will pay off in the long run.

Avoid over-complicated research designs – life is complex enough as it is without making things more difficult for yourself. Use your resources sparingly: there is no point in surveying 20 organizations if you can get a reliable result from 15. Keep returning to the research objectives to make sure you have covered everything, but also to question whether or not you are straying beyond your brief and doing things that are not central to the overall aim. In design terms, err on the side of minimalism rather than the baroque.

This economical and efficient approach not only makes best use of resources, which often means that you can offer the most attractive package to a potential sponsor or a commissioning body, it also results in a project that is likely to be easier to manage and therefore more likely to be delivered on time and within budget. Perhaps even more critically, it will be easier to analyse the research results and to draw conclusions because you have focused on the essentials. There will simply be less to distract you.

Selecting the most appropriate methods

Research methods are no more than the tools of the trade. Among some researchers, particularly within the academic community, there is an unfortunate tendency to think that research begins and ends with methodology. This is just not so.

It is important to be aware of the range of methods available and to understand how they work, appreciating their advantages and disadvantages. But you need to be able to apply that understanding to specific research problems. It is, for example, very difficult to gather much useful data about information-seeking behaviour by using self-completion questionnaires. Information is simply too diffuse and nebulous a concept to be squeezed into the constraints of that particular form of survey method. It is much better to use depth interviews or focus groups.

The essential thing is to be able to select the methods that are most likely to achieve the objectives of the research.

In general, one should beware of researchers who collect research methods like others collect stamps and who tend to regard each project as another opportunity to add to their collection. Equally dangerous are researchers who are totally committed to a single method – often one that they have devised themselves – and who try to apply it to each and every problem.

The range of basic research methods is relatively limited and it is not difficult to develop a general understanding of the most common ones. Part 2 of this book should serve as an introduction. Each method has a number of variations or can be adopted to suit different purposes. In most cases it is sufficient merely to be aware of such subtleties, learning about the detailed application as each is called for by different research projects.

Many people are hesitant about embarking on research because of the apparent complexity of the methods used, particularly those that require the use of sophisticated statistical techniques. This hesitancy is compounded by the tendency of some well-established researchers to emphasize the complexity of their craft and to build up the mystique associated with it. You should not, however, despair. It is possible to learn from experience and to begin to do research with only a partial knowledge of methods. The secret is to keep things simple and to build upon all the expertise available to you. Everyone finds it difficult to design their first questionnaire and we all benefit from advice and assistance from more experienced colleagues. It is often the case that the second questionnaire appears to be no easier than the first – simply because the pitfalls and problems are more evident – but from then on things get progressively more simple and straightforward. Once you have designed half a dozen you will be well away.

The benefits of combining methods

It is possible to enrich your results by combining methods to give an added dimension to the research. A postal questionnaire, for example, could provide a broad picture but, because of the nature of self-completion questionnaires, the results will tend to be rather superficial. This could be overcome by the use of depth interviews, or perhaps focus groups, to provide a more detailed picture of the key issues. In this way, by combining methods, you are able to provide both breadth and depth. If the design of the questionnaire and the topic list for the focus groups were preceded by a thorough review of other research on the topic, not only would you be able to learn from the experience of others but you would be able to compare your results with theirs.

You could go further and approach an issue in a number of different ways, perhaps using secondary analysis of national survey data and depth interviews with key informants and commentators as well as focus groups with service users. Each would provide a slightly different view of an issue. Together they would combine to offer a very rich picture.

The technical term for combining research methods in this way to provide a number of different views on an issue is triangulation. It is a useful concept and one that is well worth considering when designing projects as it adds considerable value to the research results.

Seven principles of selection

The job of selecting the most appropriate research methods can be made easier by following seven basic commonsense principles. If you follow these you are likely to end up with a project that stands a reasonable chance of success.

Keep things simple

This should perhaps be written in full as 'keep things simple at the beginning because they will certainly get more complicated than you expect as the work progresses.'

Begin by adopting a simple and straightforward design. Reduce things to the bare essentials required to achieve your objectives and focus on those. If you can get the basic structure right many other things will follow naturally. In that sense, good research is similar to good furniture design – functionality, simplicity and a lack of unnecessary complexity are what distinguishes the good from the bad.

Having established the overall design, try to identify methods that are themselves uncomplicated and that are within the competence of the people who will be doing the work. It is no good deciding to do econometric modelling if no-one on the team understands statistics. You may be able to buy the expertise in from outside, but you should at least be able to understand the language they will be using.

Clearly, the methods should also be commensurate with the general scale of the subject of the research. It would be counter-productive, for example, to swamp a small, poorly staffed service with a requirement for employees to keep detailed diary records of their activities.

It is also important to consider the degree of accuracy that is required. Social organizations are, at their best, imprecise organisms which are subject to numerous variables that are beyond the control of the researcher. In such circumstances it is not realistic to use methods that are designed to produce results down to two decimal places. In particular, it is simply not worth aiming for such levels of accuracy in the results if the basic data are subject to wide margins of error. Equally, it is pointless to strive for high levels of precision if the people commissioning the research are simply looking for an overall impression of the situation.

Think also about the volumes of data that you will be collecting. Large samples and lengthy questionnaires produce large quantities of data that need to be managed and input before they can be analysed. It all adds to the complexity of the research and reduces the likelihood that you will produce useful results at the end of the day.

In many cases, consider whether it would be sufficient to do what is known in the trade as a 'quick and dirty' project. These seldom produce definitive results but they can be short and focused, and often provide cost-effective answers that clear the ground for further, more detailed work later on. There is nothing intrinsically wrong with quick and dirty research, although many purists may tend to turn their noses up at it. In its place it can be effective. It is simply a case of tailoring the research to meet the needs of the situation.

All the time, err on the side of simplicity. And keep returning to the research objectives, asking continually whether what you propose to do will enable you to achieve the objectives you have been set. Concentrate on getting the essentials right and leave the non-essentials to look after themselves.

Borrow from others

One of the easiest ways to increase the likely success of a project is to borrow from others, learning from their mistakes and seeing where shortcuts can be made. As we have noted, research methods are like tools and, like any tool, they are not easy to invent or design, yet they can be used in a range of different circumstances and it is often possible to see how a slight amendment or variation could fit them perfectly for the task in hand.

So, it is always worth looking around to see if someone has done something similar before. It is always possible that the results will be transferable, providing a context within which your results can be considered. They may, indeed, save you a great deal of hard work and effort. At the very least it will be possible to learn from the approach that the other person adopted. You may be able to apply the general techniques. It is also often possible to adapt a questionnaire that has been used before, either using the whole questionnaire or borrowing individual questions. This has the added advantage that when you come to analyse your results you will have something to compare them against.

It is possible to transfer analytical techniques from one project to another and to build upon them. For some types of research this approach is almost unavoidable. In the field of performance measurement, for example, different approaches have evolved over the years and it would be a rash person who did not, to a certain degree at least, build on the work that had gone before.

Collect only what is needed

This should be engraved on the forehead of every researcher. It is probable that more projects have come to grief because they collected too much information than for any other reason.

Here it is necessary to distinguish between *wants* and *needs*. Some researchers seem to *want* an unlimited amount of information about people or the organizations they study and the problems they face. They are actually *interested* in slightly less. They can *handle*, physically and mentally, much less. In reality, they *need* only a very little.

The tendency is to think that our understanding of a problem will increase as we collect more and more information about it. In fact, the reverse is often the case. It is possible to learn a great deal about something through detailed consideration of a little carefully chosen information which relates to key issues. When more questions are asked, the amount of data increases but so, too, does the complexity and understanding often declines.

What should be avoided at all costs is the '. . . while we are about it . . .' syndrome. This is the phenomenon which pops up when someone announces that they are about to undertake a survey. Before long they think, 'While we are about it we could ask what they think of . . .' Then someone else comes along and says, 'While you are doing the survey, could you find out about . . .' Before long the questionnaire runs to 20 pages, the initial purpose of the survey is lost and the likely response rate has plummeted.

Focus, focus, focus. Concentrate on collecting information that relates only to the issues in hand. You will have a big enough job making sense of it when it all arrives without clouding the issue with other, less relevant material.

It is also possible to collect too much information by failing to select small enough samples. The marginal increase in the accuracy of a sample diminishes quite rapidly once the optimum point has been passed. Having a sample that is unnecessarily large will simply add to costs, increase the burden on respondents and increase the size of the data-handling task without adding much to your understanding of the issues or the accuracy of the results.

While, as we noted above, it is often very useful to use more than one research method to achieve breadth and depth in your results or to triangulate views on an issue, it is also possible to collect too much data by using a plethora of research methods. If using more than one, ask yourself what extra benefit you will get from the additional method. In what way will it get you closer to achieving your objectives? You should be sure that the methods genuinely complement each other and do not simply overlap.

The final point is that the amount of data collected should be constrained by the capacity of both the organization to process it and the researcher to make sense of it. All over the world, tucked under the desks of researchers, there are large piles of transcripts and computer printouts that have been looked at quickly and are waiting for that clear afternoon when it will be possible to go through them again in greater depth.

Beware the distortion that research creates

Nearly all social research distorts the subjects it seeks to study. Simply by asking people questions you are changing the environment within which they operate and altering their responses. The classic example of this is the study carried out into motivation and morale among the workers of the Hawthorne Electrical factory in the USA in the 1930s. The researchers found that morale improved simply as a result of the research taking place. The factory management did not have to do anything, simply having researchers asking questions was enough to bring about a change. From this has come the phrase 'the Hawthorne effect' to describe the fact that research sometimes changes the very thing it sets out to explore.

When selecting your methods, choose those that are least likely to intrude. In another classic case, researchers tried to find out what happened when people asked questions in a reference library. As people approached the enquiry desk, a researcher would appear and hang a tape recorder around the neck of the user and another one around the neck of the librarian. They were then told to act naturally . . .

It is, perhaps, surprising how tolerant people are. Many focus groups – on which so much seems to depend these days – take place in research suites where small groups of people who have never met each other before are brought into a tastefully furnished room. They are offered sandwiches, snacks and drinks and told that the large mirror on the wall is a two-way mirror and that behind it are three or four people from the organization commissioning the research who will observe what goes on. They are also told that tape and video recordings are being made. The strange thing is that most people who have been through the experience say that they largely forgot about the mirror and the recordings after the first few minutes. Even so, the very fact that they are put in the position of having to think hard about an issue will set them apart from their contemporaries.

Generally, the more sensitive or the more trivial an issue is, the more likely it will be that people will distort what they say. A detailed survey of sexual habits among teenagers is likely to be subject to a degree of distortion arising from bravado among the subjects. Equally a street survey of people's attitudes towards the contestants on the current reality television show is more likely to produce responses that are frivolous than serious.

It is impossible to avoid distortion altogether. All you can do is to be aware of it and to take steps to minimize its impact during the research and then to make due allowance when analysing and interpreting the results.

Use available expertise

The other essential is to draw on people's expertise and experience. If you come across a project that appears to be very similar to the one you are contemplating, get in touch with the person who carried it out and ask for their advice. Most people are really flattered to think that someone else is taking an interest in something that they probably worked hard over and they are usually very ready to offer advice on how to go about things. They may also be able to suggest improvements to the approach they adopted.

Similarly, if you are planning to use a research method with which you are not familiar, seek the advice of someone who makes regular use of the method. Ask them what you should look out for or guard against. In some cases it may be worth bringing them into the research team so that they can carry out that part of the project or work alongside you so that you undertake the task together.

If you are using outside expertise it is really important to establish a good working relationship from the outset. They may be able to contribute expertise in the use of the method. Equally, you will probably be able to contribute an understanding of the issues and the context within which the research will take place. Without such a joint approach, there is a danger that the expert will spend much time and effort establishing facts that are commonly accepted among the subject community.

In other circumstances it may be useful to involve people who know more about the subject than you do. They may be professional researchers who have specialized in the field or they may be practitioners who have a particular expertise. Either way, they should be able to add depth to the project, helping you to interpret the results and to put them into context.

It is always possible to invite experts to sit on a project advisory group. This way you will be able to borrow from their expertise during the course of the project.

Accept that some things cannot be measured

I once met a PhD student of mathematics who told me that his research involved trying to measure the area of a space that cannot be defined. In mathematical circles this is a very feasible topic for research. Outside those circles, however, few people would recognize the validity of such a task. Yet many researchers continue to spend time trying to measure phenomena that, quite simply, are unmeasurable.

It is, for example, almost impossible to measure the impact of certain things, like education, advertising or information, on individuals or on communities.

Some things can be quantified, such as the fact that people who go to university tend to earn higher salaries than those who do not. But beyond that, who is to say what the impact of a university education is on an individual? The complexities of the essential issue, the range of variables that can affect the outcome and the timescale over which the impact would need to be measured all mean that the task is almost impossible.

We should simply accept that some things are beyond our capacity to measure satisfactorily. In their place we should accept surrogates, subjective judgments or broad assessments rather than try to obtain finely graduated measurements. To do otherwise is to risk creating a spurious illusion of precision.

Cost–benefit analyses are particularly prone to this illusion of precision. It is usually possible to calculate the costs of doing something fairly precisely, although even this is not as easy as it appears at first glance. But to arrive at an estimate of the net value of the benefits that arise is something altogether different. It involves making a number of assumptions and imputing monetary values to things that people never have to spend money on, such as the time saved by improving the flow of traffic. The result is often an equation that seeks to show whether the costs are more or less than the benefits. But a change in the basis of the assumptions could change the whole balance of the conclusion.

Keep things ethical

Think about the legal and ethical issues that are involved. How, for example, will you protect people's privacy and ensure that you conform to data protection law? Normally, when you are collecting data or information from people you should assure them that the information will be kept confidential. If it will not be – perhaps because you might want to provide direct quotes in your report – you should make it clear from the outset. You might reserve the right to quote someone in a non-attributable way. But, if you do, make sure that it is not possible for an informed reader to work out who is being quoted.

If you use these seven simple principles to guide your selection of research methods, then there is a good chance that you will design a project that is within your level of competence, is focused on the most important issues and is likely to produce results that are capable of effective analysis and interpretation. You will also stand a good chance of designing a project that will be fun to do.

Using subcontractors

There is great scope for contracting out research tasks to other, more specialist organizations. Working in this way enables you to focus on your core skills and competencies and to draw on the expertise of a range of different specialists.

It is possible to subcontract almost every aspect of the research process other than the generation of the initial idea and the working out of the aim and objectives. There are companies and individuals who specialize in surveys of different kinds, in data inputting, in recruiting people to form focus groups, in drawing samples, in fact in almost everything. Many can do things more cost-effectively than you can, even when you allow for the additional costs involved in commissioning them to do the work. A fieldwork company, for example, can recruit a set of people for a focus group at a much lower cost than you could if you were doing it for the first time.

Many people find it useful to subcontract all or part of the fieldwork for a survey. How much you contract out will, clearly, depend on your preferences, your experience and the resources available to you. You could pay a company to turn your general ideas for a questionnaire or interview schedule into something professional. You could pay them to draw a sample, to undertake the mailing and receipt and to input the data. You could ask them to carry out the interviewing. They could undertake the initial processing of the data or carry out full-scale analysis to your specification.

Omnibus surveys are well worth considering. These are regular surveys carried out by social research companies, usually once each month. They survey a sample that is big enough to generate statistically valid data and they ask questions about topics that their clients specify. So, if you want to conduct a national survey to explore an issue, you do not have to go to the very considerable trouble of drawing a national sample and recruiting a field-force to do the interviewing; you simply pay to include your questions on one of the omnibus surveys. The company will help you with the phrasing of the questions and within one or two weeks you will get back fully processed results along with all the associated data about age, sex, socio-economic classification, etc of the sample.

The first step is to identify possible contractors. You can consult a trade association such as the Market Research Society, or a professional body like the Social Research Association, or ask around among your fellow researchers. Then draw up a specification setting out precisely what you want the company to do, send it out and ask for a quotation.

Do not be surprised if the prices vary widely. These variations may reveal nothing more than the fact that the companies are busy or quiet – the busier they are the higher will be the price they charge. Variations may, of course, reflect different interpretations of the specification and this is something that you must check when you discuss the work with the possible contractors. Here the onus will be on you to do all the necessary checking. You should ensure that you and the contractor are of one mind when it comes to issues like how the sample will be drawn, what sort of response rates you can expect, how much involvement you will have with the design work, what part you will play in briefing and debriefing the interviewers, how the data will be cleaned and processed, in what form the results will be presented to you and what the overall timetable will be.

Once you have decided which contractor to use, work hard to establish and maintain a close working relationship with them, ensuring that their quality is acceptable at all stages.

Many people are reluctant to subcontract work in this way. They feel that they will lose control of the research and the overall quality will suffer. In fact, subcontracting can do much to produce high quality research. You will be able to use expertise that might otherwise not be available to you. You may very well be able to extend the range and scope of your surveying, producing results that are more statistically valid. And critically, if you face tight deadlines, subcontracting may offer a way of getting through work much more quickly than if you tried to do it all yourself.

Schedule the work

Having decided what you are going to do, the next step is to decide when you are going to do it. It is perhaps here that experience counts most of all. Working out how much time to allow for different tasks and activities, and scheduling the work so that everything can be done comfortably within the duration of the project is not easy. And mistakes made here can have a big impact on the ultimate success of the project.

For some types of research you yourself will be trying to find out how much time you require. On other occasions you will have been told what the budget is and will have been given a deadline to work towards. The challenge then is to see if everything you want to do can be fitted into the time and the resources available.

Tasks

The first thing to do is to break the overall project down into a number of discrete tasks. You should aim to identify all the component parts of the work so that you can estimate how long each will take.

If, for example, you are going to carry out a project that involves a literature review, a postal survey, some focus groups, all leading to a lengthy report, you will have five main tasks – review, survey, focus groups, analysis and the report. But it will still be difficult to estimate how long each of these broad tasks will take. You will probably need to break each down further into its component parts in order to identify pieces of work that are easier to estimate. During the postal survey, for example, you will undertake ten different tasks:

- Design the questionnaire
- Pilot test the questionnaire and revise accordingly
- Assemble the mailing list
- Print the questionnaire and stuff and mail the envelopes
- Receive the returned questionnaires and log the response rate
- Issue a reminder letter
- Input the data
- Check the validity of the results
- Analyse the results
- Write the report.

You then need to take each of these tasks in turn and ask yourself how much time you will need to complete it. You can base your estimate on previous experience. If you are doing something for the first time, then you simply have to make your best estimate. One way to do this is to 'bracket' the task – ask yourself if it could be done in a day. If the answer is no, ask if you would need ten days. If you think that the answer lies somewhere in the middle, narrow things down until you arrive at a figure with which you are comfortable.

Carry on working through the process until you have estimated how many days you will require for each task.

The sequence of events

Here we introduce the second sort of time. We have calculated how many days are required for the project. Now you must think about the elapsed time in order to calculate the overall duration.

Here you need to produce a Gantt chart. This is a horizontal bar chart that graphically displays the time relationships between the different tasks in a project. The easiest way to produce one is to use a spreadsheet.

Set up the spreadsheet with the left hand column as the one in which you list all the different tasks involved in the project. The next column is for the number of days required for each task. Then, in the following columns show the number of weeks during which the project will run. Figure 2.1 overleaf shows how the spreadsheet should look at the beginning.

Then take each task in turn and work out the sequence that must be followed. Some tasks need to be completed before others can begin. For example, the pilot test of the questionnaire must await the completion of the questionnaire design. In other cases, it is possible to carry out two tasks at the same time: you can, for example, prepare the reminder letters while you are logging in the responses.

You should the list the tasks in the first column on the spreadsheet in the order in which they must be carried out. In the second column list the number of days required for each task.

You will see that the first task – designing the questionnaire – requires six days. For this, block off the next two columns to indicate that the work will take place during the first two of the project weeks. Piloting and revision requires four days and could be fitted into the third week, so block off week three in the pilot test and revise row. Carry on like this until you complete the spreadsheet. The completed Gantt chart will look like Figure 2.2 overleaf.

You will see that some tasks can be undertaken simultaneously. In other cases there are periods when you are unable to do any work. Nothing much happens in weeks six and seven. The questionnaires have been sent out and you are waiting for them to come back. Some weeks will be busier than others: during weeks 14–17 you are expecting to do 15 days of analysis, in contrast during week 13 you have only committed two days.

By examining the schedule in detail like this you can adjust the timings of tasks so that they fit in with other activities to which you are committed. You can also tighten things up. If the sponsor, or your boss, says that they want the results in 15 weeks, not 20 then you can see where it is possible to tighten up the timetable.

When planning in this way, do not fall into the trap of committing every day to the project. You will need time to do other things and you will need to build in some slack to allow for unforeseen circumstances. A strike in the local postal sorting office, for example, could introduce a delay in the receipt of completed returns. If you are working full-time on the project expect to spend about four days a week on the work itself – you will soon find that the remaining day each week gets absorbed with unforeseen activities.

Figure 2.1 *The basic Gantt chart*

Tasks	Days	1	2	3	4	5	6	7	8	Wk 9	10	11	12	13	14	15	16	17	18	19	20
Design questionnaire	6	▓	▓																		
Pilot test & revise	4			▓																	
Assemble mailing list	5				▓	▓															
Print & stuff	2					▓															
Receive & log response	3								▓	▓	▓	▓	▓								
Reminder	3									▓											
Input data	5								▓	▓	▓	▓	▓								
Check validity	2													▓							
Analyse results	15														▓	▓	▓	▓			
Write report	8																		▓	▓	▓
Total	53	3	3	4	3	4	0	0	2	4	2	1.5	1.5	2	3	4	4	4	3	3	2

Figure 2.2 *The postal survey schedule*

Milestones and deadlines

The ultimate deadline is the date when the project must be completed. To a great extent, everything needs to be worked back from that. It helps, however, to impose separate deadlines and milestones against which you can manage your progress. In our case, a milestone would be the end of week five. By this time you should have mailed out all the questionnaires and should be thinking about their receipt and analysis. Four weeks after this you should issue the reminder, and so on.

Fixed points like these give you something to work towards, against which you can measure your progress. They provide the useful function of determining when to start getting worried and when to really panic.

Calculate the cost

Once you have worked out how many days are required for the project, you are well on your way to costing it. Staff costs will almost certainly be the biggest item in the budget and, once you know how many days you require, you can easily work out how much they will cost.

There are two main approaches to calculating the cost of staff time. Most academic institutions appoint staff on fixed-term contracts to work on single research projects. Thus, if a project calls for 120 days of a research assistant they would appoint someone for seven or eight months. The staff costs in this instance are the salary costs plus the costs of staff insurance and possibly a pension contribution.

That approach has, however, been found to be rather imprecise. It certainly does not provide sufficient information with which to manage the time effectively and it breaks down almost entirely when research staff are required to work on more than one project at a time. To overcome these problems, many academic institutions are moving over to the tighter system which is common among consultancies and independent research institutes. Here, everything is costed according to the number of research days required. Under this system it becomes possible to calculate the cost of a project much more precisely. It is also much easier to manage programmes of research which require staff to work on more than one project at any one time.

The first step towards costing on the basis of the daily rates is to calculate what the daily rate should be. To do this, first calculate the total salary cost, plus insurance and pensions if required. This gross annual cost then needs to be divided by the number of productive days that can be undertaken by that research worker. If you start with 365 days, subtract 104 for weekends, subtract a further 10–15 for public holidays and a further 18–25 for annual holidays (depending on the practice within your institution). This will leave approximately 225 days.

Make an allowance for the person being taken ill – ten days is not unusual. And allow about a day a month for general administration, training and so on. You will then be down to about 200 days in a year. This is about the maximum that it is reasonable to expect anyone to spend working on contracted research projects.

If you expect the researcher to spend time writing proposals, undertaking general dissemination activities and getting out and about, then the expectation of 200 contract days needs to be reduced accordingly. A senior researcher in charge of a research programme and a number of research staff might expect to spend three or four days a month on these external activities and so their annual expectation would be closer to 150 days.

Divide the total annual salary cost by the number of days you expect the researcher to work and you get their cost per day. If the project is likely to run for a year or more, remember to make allowance for any salary increases that might take place.

To get a full cost per day, you need to add on the organizational overhead. This is the amount the organization has to spend simply to keep the place ticking over. In independent institutions, the overhead is likely to be about 100 per cent of salary. In academic institutions it will be less as most governments subsidize universities so that they can carry out research. In Britain, most universities charge a 40 per cent overhead on research grants.

Why not work out how much you cost for each productive day you work? Take your annual salary, add on the employer's contributions to insurance and pensions – in Britain this usually adds 20 per cent to the basic salary cost. Divide the total by 200 and multiply by two to allow for the full overhead cost. That's how much each of your productive days cost. Bet you never knew you were that valuable – or expensive.

So, if you know how many days you require and you have calculated the daily rate for the job, you can work out what the staff costs will be.

Calculating the other costs is usually a matter of the careful application of common sense. Work through each of the research tasks and ask yourself how much they will cost. If you are planning to send out 200 questionnaires, you will need to print about 300 copies of the questionnaire itself to allow for reminders. You will need 200 letters and 400 envelopes with 400 stamps as you will need to provide a stamped addressed envelope for people to return the completed questionnaire. Then you will need 100 reminder letters with a further 200 envelopes and stamps. Simply think things through methodically, adding up the costs as you go.

Ask yourself if there will be any travelling. How many visits and how far will you go? Will you need to stay overnight?

If you need to use a fieldwork company, get them to give you a clear indication of what the costs will be. Ensure that it is a fixed quotation rather than an estimate that could be varied later. Check whether it includes Value Added Tax.

In some cases, sponsors allow you to include the cost of capital items like computers and tape recorders. Not unreasonably, many sponsors claim ownership of these items at the end of the research.

Equally, sponsors vary in their attitudes towards dissemination of the results. Some are keen to see vigorous dissemination built into the proposal for research and are happy to cover the costs. Others take a different view and expect you to cover most of the costs of dissemination. Check what the position is before finalizing your costs.

As with the calculation of research time, err on the side of caution and make allowances for unforeseen circumstances. It is better to have a little money left over at the end of a project than to run out halfway through.

By this stage you will probably be beginning to think that actually doing the research is the easy bit. But do not despair. It sounds complicated but, if you approach the task of designing and planning research systematically and carefully, and if you keep things simple from the outset, it is really not difficult. And if you plan in detail at the beginning, you will find it so much easier to manage the work once it gets under way.

SUMMARY

The size and shape of the research project will be determined by the constraints of money, time and expertise. When thinking about time consider two different sorts: elapsed time between the start and finish of the project and the number of research days required to carry out the work. Aim for a design that is simple, efficient and economical.

Select the research methods that are most likely to enable you to achieve your research objectives. Combining methods can enrich the picture you obtain from your research. Be guided in your selection by seven basic principles:

- Keep things simple
- Borrow from others
- Collect only what is needed
- Beware the distortion that research creates
- Use available expertise

- Accept that some things cannot be measured.
- Keep things ethical.

Schedule the work so that you have a clear idea of what you need to do and when you need to do it. Break the overall task down into smaller tasks so that you can estimate fairly accurately how many research days each will require. Use a Gantt chart to specify the sequence of activities and to identify precisely when each task will take place. Identify milestones and deadlines that will help you to monitor the progress of the work.

Calculate the costs of the project by first establishing the cost of the staff time involved. The best way to do this is by calculating a daily rate, or the cost of a productive day's research. Use this to work out the total cost of research staff. Then, taking each task in turn, calculate how much money will be required.

If you approach these tasks systematically and carefully, and if you keep things simple, you will have created the framework within which you can manage a successful project.

3
Write the proposal

Just as a builder requires a detailed set of plans to guide the building of a house, so a researcher needs a proposal to help structure and manage the research project. Too often, the proposal is regarded as an inconvenience that is only required in order to obtain external funds for a project or to obtain approval for an academic dissertation. It is thought to be something that can be discarded once the funds have been allocated or the approval given. This is a very limited view of research proposals. Those who take it leave themselves without one of the most useful tools for managing research.

Research proposals, in fact, play a number of important rôles in the research process and, while preparing a proposal may seem like a distraction or an unnecessary waste of time, the work involved should ensure that you think through all the aspects concerned with the project before the research itself begins to take over. Because once the project starts rolling it is often too late to begin making changes and adjustments that would have been obvious in advance if the project had been properly prepared.

The purposes of research proposals

Proposals have a number of different purposes. A small in-house project will clearly require a less complicated proposal than a major project for which external funds are being sought. But the purposes they serve will, by and large, be the same.

To gain the approval of a supervisor

The proposal plays an important rôle in justifying the research to a supervisor. It is the vehicle that you use to argue the case for the research, demonstrating that it is important that you are capable of undertaking – and successfully completing – the work, and that the work will enable you to achieve the educational objectives of the exercise.

For academic research projects, you will need to obtain your supervisor's approval for your ideas at an early stage. You will need to be able to show that you have a clear understanding of the general issues and theories associated with the topic that you wish to study. You should be able to cite the key authors in the field and you should be able to demonstrate how your approach fits with the research that others have carried out.

The proposal should begin with a small essay setting the scene, establishing the context of the work and specifying the theoretical framework within which you will be working.

Having established the case for the research, you then need to specify precisely what it is that you will be exploring. This is where the aim and objectives come in. You may be proposing to test an hypothesis, in which case, this is where you set out the basis for the hypothesis and outline how you will test it. The supervisor should be left in no doubt about what you are going to do and why. This will enable them to assess the likely scale of the work and judge whether it is too ambitious or too small in scale to warrant the eventual award of a degree.

The supervisor will also be looking for the research methods that you propose to use. They will need to be assured not only that the methods are likely to achieve the aim and objectives, but also that you have the skills required to deploy the techniques successfully. Once again, they will need to be able to assess the likely scale of the project and whether it fits with the scale of resources at your disposal.

At a slightly different level, this is your opportunity to catch the supervisor's interest. In the months or years to come you will be working fairly closely with your supervisor, asking them for support and for informed comment. If you can excite their interest from the outset you stand a good chance of making it a more productive and enjoyable relationship.

To obtain approval from the organization

If you are employed as a researcher within an organization, and are asked to carry out a piece of research, it is good practice to produce a brief proposal in order to obtain formal approval for the work. This may seem to be an unnecessary obligation, as you are simply responding to a request from above, but you should regard it as the first step in the process of conducting a piece of research that will be accepted by the organization.

To begin with, the proposal will ensure that you have interpreted your brief correctly. It should set out your assumptions and provide you with clear aims and objectives. It will also give the organization a clear understanding of the scale and nature of the resources involved.

Once you have received formal approval for the work, you can use the proposal as a means of explaining the purpose of the research to others within the organization, particularly those who will be affected by the research process and by the results.

The proposal will also provide you with a bit of security. Research has the irritating tendency to produce results that people did not expect. In such cases, the inclination is often to try to question, or even to discredit, the research. If you are armed with an agreed proposal, you are in a much stronger position to defend your results.

To obtain financial support

Obtaining funds from an external sponsor is, in essence, not that different from obtaining approval from a research supervisor. You have to argue the case for the award of money and you have to show that you will make good use of the funds when you get them.

The funder will almost certainly consult external referees who will be asked to comment on the need for the research, the validity of the aim and objectives, the methods proposed and the resources required. These referees will only have the proposal on which to base their judgments. It is, therefore, vital that it answers all the possible questions that they might raise and that it provides them with sufficiently detailed information on which to base their judgments.

The trick is to look at a draft of the proposal imagining that you are a sceptical referee. Ask all the difficult questions you can think of – like, how big will the sample be? What response rates are they expecting? How will they analyse the data? What experience will they bring to the project? In the light of your responses to these questions, consider whether you need to revise the proposal. Most people find that they need to add more detail to the section on methods. If you feel really brave, give the proposal to an experienced colleague and ask them to pick holes in it.

The proposal must demonstrate that the work clearly falls within the terms of reference of the funding body. This is the first hurdle and a surprising number of proposals fail to clear it.

Nearly all funders provide very clear guidance on the kinds of research they will support and the subject areas in which they are interested. It is simply a waste of everyone's time and effort to produce and submit proposals to organizations that are not empowered to fund them. This seems self-evident, yet it is surprising how many researchers begin the long process of obtaining financial support by, in effect, attempting to persuade the funder to alter its terms of reference. If you find yourself having difficulty justifying the research in terms of the funder's priorities, then think twice about proceeding further.

For an organization to commit funds to a project, it must be convinced of the need for the research. This should come out very clearly in the proposal. Evidence of need can come from recommendations made in previous research projects, from the general literature, from official reports, from practitioners or even from the results of a quick-and-dirty study. Whichever source is used, it should be documented and cited in full. If a key document is unlikely to be easy for the funder to obtain, perhaps because it was an internally circulated report, then it is often worth enclosing a copy with the proposal.

Also important is the need to show how the proposed research fits with other research on related topics. You might be aware of other work in progress in a related field on which you could draw, or you may argue that your work is needed to support or refute a controversial finding. Most funders recognize the incremental nature of development and like to see how they would be complementing or building on work that has gone before. This not only adds value to the previous and proposed research, it may also suggest economies in the design of your project. Be careful, though, that in stressing the closeness of these links, you do not open yourself to the criticism that you will be reinventing the wheel.

Funding agencies seldom want to take undue risks with their money. Indeed, in many cases, they are charged with spending public money or are required by their charitable status to act prudently. They therefore need to be convinced that the researcher is likely to spend their money wisely. This means that the proposal must demonstrate familiarity with the topic, the proposed methods and any related developments – remember that they would rather grant-aid an expert than an amateur. Use the proposal to show your level of expertise, mentioning the previous research you have undertaken, the supporting expertise within your organization and your general standing in the field.

Closely related to the desire to obtain value for money is the desire to ensure that the research has a general relevance or applicability. Few funders will support work that is the sole concern of a single organization or even a small group of organizations. The funder will be looking for opportunities to do the greatest good for the largest number. So stress the general relevance and applicability and show how you will bring the results to the attention of all those who could act on them.

This brings us to dissemination. Just about every project produces a report. Many go no further and the results are entombed in what is often a formal document that is not widely circulated and seldom read even by those who receive a copy. If you believe in the importance of your research, this should not be enough for you. Use the proposal to show how you will write articles, give conference papers, go on television and arrange seminars to communicate the results of your research to as many people as possible or, more sensibly, to a number of clearly targeted audiences.

The funder will, not unreasonably, want to know what you plan to spend the money on. The costing in the proposal should be clear and as detailed as possible. The actual format for presenting the costings will almost certainly be determined by the funder. If it differs widely from the basis that you use to calculate the costs, then it is quite acceptable to show both approaches to demonstrate that you have thought things through carefully. Make sure, though, that the total costs are the same with both approaches.

Make clear what is included and what excluded. Many funders place a limit on the level of organizational overheads they will accept. Clearly you have to conform to this and if the funder will not cover the full costs it is quite justifiable to indicate clearly the contribution that will be made by your organization. For projects that extend over more than a year, establish clearly how you will deal with any inflation. Some funders will automatically accept, for example, nationally agreed salary awards without you having to specify them. If they do not, you will have to forecast what such awards will be and make the necessary allowance when calculating your costs.

Finally, have a thought about cash flow. The funder will almost certainly have an established procedure for giving you the money. Most expect you to do the work and then reclaim the costs in arrears, usually on a quarterly basis. Some will pay in equal instalments, others require you to detail the actual costs that have been incurred. It is worth making sure that your organization can cover this kind of cash flow requirement. It is also worth making an allowance for any large payments that may be required. If, for example, you are using a fieldwork company, you may be faced with a large bill at some stage in the project. It might be possible to negotiate with the funder so that you receive payment in advance to cover this large cash outlay.

The proposal also provides the basis for accountability. Sometimes it becomes part of the contract between the funding body and the researcher. As such it will be used by the funder to monitor progress and to ensure that its funds are being spent prudently. It is therefore important that the proposal provides the basis for this monitoring. It should contain a detailed timetable and it should identify clearly the milestones and deadlines that will mark the progress of the work. Any major changes that are made during the course of the work should, naturally, be communicated to the funder.

Finally the proposal should indicate the extent of the contribution that the applicant will make to the costs of the project. If you are applying as an individual, even a small contribution will serve as an indication of the strength of your commitment. It need not be a contribution in cash terms. It could be an offer to organize a dissemination event in your own time, or a suggestion that you explore a related issue outside the strict confines of the proposed work.

It is easier to make a contribution when the proposal is being submitted by an organization. The contribution can be in cash or in kind. The organization could offer to support a particular aspect of the work, perhaps meeting the cost of some focus groups or supporting a seminar to discuss the interim results. Or they could offer to provide technical expertise to support the research workers. Every little helps to indicate the commitment of the applicant.

Remember always that you are producing something that will act as an ambassador for you and your ideas in the hope that someone will hand over quite a large amount of money. So make sure the proposal looks good. Pay attention to the layout and the design, make sure all the figures add up and that there are no typos or drafting errors. Most good research requires a meticulous approach and your proposal should demonstrate that this is just what you are capable of.

To demonstrate competence

Whether the proposal is justifying a piece of research leading to an academic qualification or supporting an application for funds, it must demonstrate that you are capable of doing the work satisfactorily.

The proposal provides you with the opportunity to display your under-standing of the subject, your awareness of the associated issues and your familiarity with the necessary research techniques. You should use the oppor-tunity to the full.

Every proposal should have something about you and your organization in it. This is often the most difficult bit to write as you need to sell yourself and, for most of us, this does not come easily. But put your natural modesty aside. Try to look at yourself dispassionately and produce a statement that will convince a potential supervisor or funder. Start by recognizing that the very fact that you are interested in the topic is an indication of your commitment, if nothing else. Draw on your past experience. If you have not done much research before, exploit your work experience or, at the very least, show that you have read widely and have studied research methods in the abstract if not in practice.

Do not, however, claim more than is justifiable – if the supervisor or funder does not catch you out before you begin the project, rest assured that they will do so by the end.

As a basis for planning

Writing a research proposal forces you to think through what you plan to do. This is probably the most important function of research proposals. Because of this, it is always worth writing a proposal even if you do not have to justify yourself to a supervisor, to your employer or to a funder. If you embark on a research project without going through the kind of planning process that is required by a formal proposal, then you are embarking on a very uncertain enterprise.

The proposal should put the work into context, forcing you to consider explicitly the events and conditions leading to the project, the need for it and the relevance of other work in related fields. To do this properly will almost certainly call for a little investigation: at the very least, you should conduct a small literature search to check that you have not missed anything recently published and a check of research registers to make sure no-one else is engaged on an identical study.

Consider also how the work fits into the overall development of your organization. Will it take you into new areas, or will it be building on work you have done previously?

All this will lead to the statement of the research aim and the objectives.

The proposal should contain a full statement of the methods to be used. Again the discipline of producing the proposal ensures that you think through what you are going to do, ideally assessing the effectiveness of one approach against others before settling on the ones that are most likely to enable you to achieve your objectives economically.

The proposal should contain a detailed statement of the resources required for the research and some kind of justification for them. If you plan to spend £1000 on travel and subsistence, for example, you should be prepared to give some kind of rationale for the amount. Once again, it is the discipline imposed by having to commit something to paper that is important in forcing you to think things through in advance.

Similarly the proposal should cover the schedule of work, noting how you will cope with busy periods and identifying milestones and deadlines against which you will monitor your progress.

All this is necessary when seeking approval for a project or when soliciting funds for research. But it is a process that is well worth going through even if you will be undertaking the work from your own resources. You may not think it at the time when you are writing the proposal, but you will be grateful that you did it when you are two-thirds of the way through the research.

As a framework for managing the research

In nearly every research project there comes a time when you begin to feel rather lost. On the one hand you feel overwhelmed by the complexity and magnitude of the issue you are dealing with – you cannot see how anyone could ever get to grips with it. On the other, the whole thing seems so trivial and self-evident that you cannot understand why you ever thought it needed a research project in the first place and you might as well shut up shop and go home.

Do not despair. Just about everyone goes through this. Dig out the proposal and use it to put everything back into context. Look again at the rationale for the work, why it is important. Remind yourself what you are trying to achieve by studying the aim and objectives again. Use the statement of methods to reassure yourself that you are, in fact, doing something useful that is designed to bring you closer to your objectives. Look at the timetable and panic. It all helps to put everything back into place and to set you up for the remainder of the project.

Most professional researchers find themselves returning again and again to the proposal when the research is in progress. It provides a framework within which they manage the research. It will not necessarily overcome the feeling of being lost two-thirds of the way into the project, but it will help keep the research moving smoothly, on-time and within budget.

Much depends on the scale of the project. If you are working on the research by yourself, you will find it helpful to refer regularly to the proposal to structure and manage your work, to check that you have made the required amount of progress and, if you have not, to identify how you can best get back on track.

If you are working on a bigger project, perhaps one that involves a number of research workers, the proposal provides the basis for developing a common understanding of what you are all trying to achieve. All staff recruited to work on the project should be given a copy of the proposal and should be encouraged to use it as a basic reference tool.

As the work comes to a conclusion, the proposal provides the starting point for interpreting the results and putting them into context. It may seem odd, but at this stage in a project it is not always easy to remember exactly what it is that you set out to do – so many interesting snippets of information will have come to light and the initial issue, which seemed so straightforward at the time, will probably now appear much more complex. The proposal will remind you of what it was you first intended to achieve. The aim and objectives will help you to develop the analytical framework that you will need to make sense of all those pages of computer printout or all the interview scripts.

Then when you come to assemble everything for the report, the proposal, or more properly, the aim and objectives, will provide the starting point for developing the report's structure. As a minimum, you will need to check that you have, in fact, addressed each of the objectives. The proposal should also remind you of the audience, or audiences, to which you are addressing the report.

·All in all, the proposal provides a means of ensuring that the wood does not become obscured by the trees.

The structure of research proposals

A good thing to begin with is a title. This should be sufficiently precise to indicate the nature and scope of the project but concise enough to be referred to quickly and easily throughout the course of the work. You will probably need to use it on questionnaires and other documents such as press releases. It is worth spending a little time trying to find something that meets these very different requirements. If all else fails, pick a snappy title and support it with an explanatory subtitle.

Let us use as an example a proposal that Adrienne Muir and I prepared when we worked together at the Policy Studies Institute. We wanted to explore the changing employment market for information professionals, looking at the extent to which changes in the ways that organizations used information had altered the demand for librarians and other information specialists. The title we chose was *The market for information professionals*. It is concise and it describes the nature and scope of the research quite precisely. (The full proposal is included as an example in the Appendix on page 163.)

Introduction or background

The first substantial section of the proposal will be the introduction. This is where you describe the background to the study, setting the scene for the work and putting it into context. It is usual to trace the historical development of the issue and to cite fully all the other relevant work on which your research will build.

The introduction should also be sufficiently appealing to awaken the interest of referees, research funders and potential recruits to the research team. Aim to make the introduction easy to read and to understand. You are producing something that has to capture the attention of people who probably have little background in the subject, and who will not necessarily understand the significance of some things that are self-evident to you as an interested expert.

At the same time, you need to be able to convey your authority as an expert in the field or, at least, as someone who has given considerable thought to the issue and who is familiar with the main developments and all the significant research in the area.

This is also the section where you make the case for the research. You need to argue convincingly that the research is important and that your study will either shed light on the issue so that people can take action as a result or, alternatively, that you will be able to advance our theoretical understanding of the issue. Remember that, in either case, you are trying to persuade people to give away money – they have to be convinced that it is for a worthwhile cause.

You should demonstrate that you are aware of all other relevant research and writing on the subject. Try to make allowance for the kind of pedantic referee who delights in pointing out that your list of references does not include the article on the subject published in an obscure journal ten years ago. In particular, show that you are aware of other relevant research that is currently taking place and indicate how your study will be complementary.

If possible, indicate the likely audiences for the research results. Ask yourself who is affected by the issue that you are going to study, and who is likely to be in a position to take some kind of action based on the results.

The introductory section of the example in the appendix adopts an historical approach. This was very important in this particular case as the research proposed to explore the changes that had taken place during the ten years that had passed since a previous study explored the issue. It also tries to put the work into an international context to show that the issue is one of broad interest.

Statement of aim and objectives

The introduction should lead naturally on to the statement of the aim and objectives. In our example, we have a nice, clear, unambiguous sentence that encapsulates what the research is all about:

> The aim of the study is to identify the range of skills that will be required by future information professionals.

The proposal goes on to qualify this by stating very briefly how we will approach the issue:

> We will do this by exploring the range of skills, qualifications and experience required by employers of information professionals in the late 1990s; assessing the extent to which these requirements have changed over the last ten years and comparing the requirements with the characteristics of people applying for such positions.

This gives anyone reading the proposal a taste of what is to come and helps to fix the overall approach in their mind. It also serves to lead into the statement of the research objectives:

Within this overall aim, therefore, the study has three specific objectives:

- To analyse the range and nature of the skills required by employers who are actively recruiting information professionals and to identify the extent to which employers are able to satisfy their requirements
- To assess the extent to which people recruited to jobs as information professionals meet the employers' requirements and from this to assess the relevance of education and training provision
- To explore with both employers and employees the ways in which skill requirements are likely to develop in the future.

Anyone reading the proposal should now have a clear idea about why the research is necessary and precisely what it is setting out to achieve.

Statement of methods

The next section deals with the methods to be used. Here it is worth noting that the proper term for this section is 'methods' – 'methodology' is the study of research methods.

This is the part of the proposal that most often presents people with difficulties. It is also the bit that referees are likely to spend most time reviewing. If, however, you have approached the design and planning of the research systematically, all you will need to do is to find the best form of words to describe what you intend to do.

Much of what follows in the proposal will depend on the methods chosen and if it is not possible to describe with confidence what you propose to do, then that makes it difficult for anyone to place much credibility in the whole proposal.

Let us assume that you have carefully selected the combination of methods that will best enable you to achieve your objectives. What you now have to do is to provide sufficient detail about what you propose to enable a sceptical referee to judge first, whether you are capable of bringing it all off and secondly, whether the approach chosen is likely to achieve the objectives.

Again, it is useful to try to look at it from the perspective of the referee. What would you want to know? What would you expect to see in the proposal?

You need to justify your choice of methods, indicating clearly how they relate to the objectives. You need to give sufficient detail about things like sample sizes to enable the referee to judge your competence and to show that your costings are based on more than simple guesswork. If possible you need to anticipate potential problems and say how you plan to overcome them. If you are using more than one method, state clearly how they relate to one another.

If in doubt, provide additional detail. Even if the referees skim over it, you will find it useful in the long run, not least because it will give those working with you a clearer idea about what is going on. Everyone recognizes that adaptations may be necessary during the research but they expect you to have a well thought-out plan at the outset.

Remember also that dissemination should be included in the statement of methods.

Turning to our example of research into the market for information professionals, you will see that it proposes the use of a technique that was used successfully in the past, thus providing an opportunity to compare results with those obtained earlier. The technique will be adapted and the proposal indicates how this will be done. A fair amount of detail is provided about the size of the study. To enrich the survey results a number of round-table meetings will be held to discuss the results with groups of experts. Finally there is a paragraph about dissemination.

Statement of timescale

The next section sets out the programme for the work. This could be done by presenting the Gantt chart or, as in our appended example, by simply listing the main tasks and stating when they will be undertaken. One thing that is missing from our example is a list of the milestones that could be used to monitor progress.

Statement of who will do the work

This section can usefully be divided into two. In many cases it is appropriate first to provide information about the organization within which the work will be carried out. This is particularly important if the research is to be based in a research-orientated organization. The context within which the research takes place is important. Success is more likely if there is a supporting research culture and if the researchers have access to expert colleagues and to a system for managing research.

The second section covers the research staff – the people who will actually be doing the work. Here it is normal to provide a brief biography describing the individuals, followed by a statement of their rôle in the whole project. In some cases, particularly for research which is more academic in nature, it is common to provide a full curriculum vitae.

In some cases the project will be staffed by researchers recruited for the purpose. In this case you cannot describe their attributes or provide their curriculum vitae. Instead you should make it clear that you intend to recruit and provide a fairly detailed specification of the kind of person that you are looking for. But be realistic. Do not claim that you will be able to recruit someone with five or more years' research experience, good statistical and analytical skills and sufficient poise and self-confidence to conduct depth interviews with key informants, but only have to pay them on the bottom of the scale.

You may also plan to involve an advisory committee to oversee the work. If so, this is the place in the proposal to mention it. Indicate the rôle that you expect the advisory group to fulfil and suggest the types of people that you expect to invite.

Statement of costs

This is where you have to commit yourself. If you get the costings wrong you may well find that you end up with fewer resources than you need to get the job done satisfactorily. Most funders will expect to see a fairly detailed statement of what the costs are and how they have been calculated. In contrast, other funders, often those in the academic sphere, require more general statements of costs and assume, for example, that the staff employed on the project will work on it more or less full-time. Not for them the detailed statements of the numbers of research days required for individual tasks.

In the appended example, you will see that we give a general breakdown of costs under four broad headings. Slightly more detail was given on the actual application form. What is not shown here is the detailed calculation of the number of days required for each of the specific research tasks. It is a case of presenting the information in the form required by the funder.

If in doubt, err on the side of detail. Provide a full statement of your assumptions and of the time you expect to spend on each task in terms of both research days and elapsed time. Only by doing this can you be clear in your own mind that you are being honest with the funder when you ask them for some of their money.

The other advantage of setting things out in detail is that you then have a basis for negotiation if the funder comes back and says that they like the project but the amount requested is too large. In the example of the proposal for the research into the market for information professionals, the total cost comes to £29,950. The funder has no basis for judging what the impact would be if they asked you to reduce the budget to £25,000. In contrast, a fully itemized costing would enable them to see the impact of a reduction in expenditure, or at least, it would give you a starting point for negotiating an agreed settlement.

Finally, it might be useful to indicate how the expenditure will be spread over the duration of the project and, in particular, how it falls into different financial years.

Presentation

I referred earlier to the need to present the proposal professionally. It should be stressed again here. A well laid-out proposal that looks as if it has been assembled with care and precision will create a much better impression than one that looks as if it has been thrown together on the way to work that morning.

Adapting the basic structure

There will be occasions when you will feel the need to change this basic structure. Proposals submitted by commercial research agencies, for example, usually begin with a fairly substantial section outlining the strengths of the organization and arguing that it is the one best placed to do the work. You might also find it useful to have a section setting out what the outcomes of the research will be, going beyond the basic report to include journal articles, discussion papers, in fact any tangible products that will result from the research activity.

The secret is to be aware of the primary purpose of the proposal – whether to obtain finance, to be endorsed by your employer, to obtain approval from an academic supervisor or to serve as a framework for planning and managing the research – and then to adapt the basic structure accordingly. One thing is certain – few proposals will omit any of the sections identified here.

SUMMARY

Proposals have a number of different purposes. You can use a proposal to justify the research to a supervisor. It is the vehicle that you use to argue the case for the research, demonstrating that it is important and that you are capable of undertaking the work.

43

For in-house researchers, the proposal ensures that everyone concerned understands the aim, objectives and resource implications of the work.

On other occasions, the proposal provides the basis for obtaining financial support for your research. You have to argue the case for the award of money and you have to show that you will make good use of the funds when you get them.

The proposal should demonstrate your competence. It should show that you understand the subject in general and the issue to be researched in particular. It should also indicate that you are familiar with the research techniques you propose to use.

Writing a proposal forces you to plan the work carefully and makes you think through each stage before you begin. And once started, it provides the framework within which you can manage the project. Even when a proposal is not required by a funder or a supervisor, it is worth going through the process.

Most proposals follow a common structure. You can vary it to suit different needs and circumstances, but the basic structure will be sufficient for most purposes.

You need to begin with a title that is both concise and precise. The proposal itself begins with an introductory section. This is where you make the case for undertaking the research, justifying its importance. The introduction also sets the scene, putting the work into context. This is where you demonstrate your understanding of the issues.

The aim and objectives should flow naturally from the introduction. In turn, they lead into the statement of methods. This should be fairly full, justifying your choice of methods and providing referees with enough detail to enable them to form an opinion about your ability to carry out the work satisfactorily. The methods section is followed by the timescale, setting out the overall programme and identifying milestones and deadlines.

You need a section giving information about who will carry out the work. This may also include a note about the organization within which the project will be based.

The proposal should conclude with a statement of costs. Here you should provide sufficient detail to reassure the funder that their money will be spent prudently.

Finally, the proposal should look good. It should inspire confidence in your ability to work carefully and constructively, paying attention to detail.

4
Obtain financial support for the research

Most people start doing research as a requirement of an academic course or as part of their job. And for many, this will be sufficient experience of research. If the process appeals to you, however, you will probably be looking for a wider range of research opportunities and, before long, you will find yourself in a position where you need to obtain external finance to support your research.

External funding comes in two main forms, depending on who has the idea for the research. Either you have an idea for a research project which you then take to a possible funder, or the funder announces that they want to commission a particular piece of research and you submit a proposal. Each form calls for a slightly different approach.

The sources of responsive funding

In most countries there is a fairly wide range of organizations that have been established to finance research or that have research funding as part of their brief.

Academic research councils

The best known funders are the research councils. They exist to channel government money through to the academic community and, to this extent, they serve as an explicit acknowledgment of the central rôle that research plays in higher education.

In Britain there are several research councils. Social research funds are channelled through the Economic and Social Research Council which each year spends almost £100 million supporting research in the higher education sector. It receives a large number of applications from academic researchers putting forward their ideas for research. These are refereed and, subject to approval by the referees and the availability of funds, the award is made to the applicant's institution. The grants are usually quite substantial – most are for more than £50,000.

The Economic and Social Research Council, in common with most research councils, tries to encourage and support new researchers. To do this, it supports training in research techniques and has set aside a fund for small grants to be made to people who have not received a research council grant before. Applications made under this scheme are treated more quickly and in a slightly less bureaucratic manner than those for larger grants.

As well as the open application procedure, the Council has a range of research programmes focused on particular topics or subjects. In these cases the Council announces the programme, appoints a coordinator and asks for proposals to undertake work within the general scope of the programme. The budgets for the programmes can be quite large – often running into millions of pounds – but because the subject matter is constrained, the competition for funds tends to be less severe.

The Council also supports a number of research centres. Here it provides long-term finance to an institute to enable it to undertake a programme of research into an issue. Research centre status is highly desired within the academic community as it can provide financial security for five or ten years – a luxury indeed in the uncertain world of contract research.

Most other developed countries have similar arrangements.

Charities and foundations

Many charitable trusts and foundations support research. The biggest in Britain is the Wellcome Trust that spends about £400 million each year, mainly on medical research. Few, however, are anything like as big; indeed many only have a few thousand pounds available to support research.

These charities and foundations have been established to support work in particular areas. Some have fairly general terms of reference – the Joseph Rowntree Foundation, for example, 'supports a wide programme of research and development projects in the fields of housing, social care and disability, young people and families, and work, income and social policy. There are smaller programmes on local government and the voluntary sector.' Others are much more specific.

Their procedures for dealing with research applications vary considerably. The big ones have well established systems into which aspiring researchers have to fit their applications. The smaller ones tend to be rather more flexible, often asking for an informal approach to be made to the secretary or director of the trust in the first instance.

The first thing you need to do if you are thinking of approaching a trust or foundation is to check one of the published directories to find out which bodies are likely to support research in the area in which you are interested. In Britain there is a website – www.trustfunding.org.uk – which lists over 4200 grant-making trusts with a total of over £3.1 billion a year to dispense. It has taken over from the *Directory of Grant-making Trusts* and is now the best-known listing of charities and foundations. It enables you to search by subject and it gives details of the amounts of money available and where to get further information. Similar publications exist in most countries that have a thriving charitable sector.

Public sector organizations

A number of public bodies have research funds that are open to unsolicited applications.

They usually work in ways that are modelled on those of the research councils. However, it is more normal for public bodies, when they support research, to work to their own agenda, issuing calls for tender to support work that they have identified as being important.

Commercial sponsorship

There is increasing scope for obtaining commercial sponsorship for research. Much, however, depends on the prevailing culture. In the United States of America, for example, there is a long established tradition of corporate donation and many companies give considerable sums to worthwhile causes, including research. In other countries, such as Britain, corporate philanthropy is less common. It is true that many of the major foundations were established by industrialists – the Leverhulme Trust, the Wellcome Trust, the Joseph Rowntree Foundation, the Nuffield Trust – all were created when the men who bore their names came towards the end of their lives and endowed the foundations with their fortunes. Until recently, however, it was less common for corporations to use some of their annual profits for charitable purposes.

For various reasons, charitable donation has been encouraged in recent years and commercial sponsorship offers an additional potential source of funds for aspiring researchers. As with charities and foundations, the secret is to do the background research to discover which companies are most likely to be interested in your research idea and then to approach one or two, rather than firing off letters to a large number in the hope that one will respond positively. Check the company website or its annual report. Look for the corporate affairs department and see whether they have in the past supported anything resembling the type of project you have in mind. If you are lucky, you will identify a potential source.

You then have to look at your proposition from their point of view. Few corporations are truly altruistic. Most receive many more applications than they can support from the funds they have available and, quite naturally, they are more inclined to support projects that produce some form of benefit for the company. They will sponsor an orchestral performance, for example, because they can use the opportunity to entertain their important clients and because the company name will be prominently displayed on the posters and the programmes. You have to ask yourself what you can offer that will generate benefits like this.

Consortium funding

Sources of research funds are always limited and it is not always possible to persuade one funder to meet the full cost of your project. In such circumstances you can, quite legitimately, seek support from more than one sponsor with a view to setting up a consortium. Do, however, make sure that everyone knows that this is what you have in mind.

The trick is to get one organization to commit funds first and then to use their support as a means of levering money out of others. The initial commitment can serve as evidence that your idea has credibility and the backing of at least one body. This is often particularly effective if the sponsors come from both the public and the private sectors.

But, be warned. Assembling a funding consortium can be both time-consuming and problematic. Clearly, you increase the amount of time spent approaching and negotiating with sponsors. You can also run into conflicts between the requirements of the different bodies. One may, for example, want you to start the work immediately in order to fit the expenditure into the current financial year, while another may not be in a position to give you an answer until their grants committee meets in two months' time. Reconciling such differences can be a headache.

Approaching the funder

Let us assume that you have a brilliant idea for a piece of research. You have done the initial design work and planning and know what kind of research you want to carry out and you have a pretty good idea of how much money you need. What do you do next?

Identifying the best source

First you have to consider which funder is the most appropriate for your project.

If your research is academic, your options are relatively straightforward. You can approach a research council or possibly one of the more academically inclined foundations. Those looking for funding for applied research face a wider range of choices. There are hundreds of foundations to choose from and similar numbers of corporations that might be persuaded to sponsor you. You need to reduce the options to a manageable number.

Check all the relevant directories to produce an initial long-list of potential sources. Then do your homework on them. Look at their websites, ask for published guidelines, examine past annual reports to get a feeling for the types of projects they support. Get hold of copies of the application forms and consider how your project would fit. Above all, study the terms of reference and make sure your project is central to the sponsor's interests. And that you are eligible for an award – some foundations, for example, are only empowered to award grants to charitable bodies. You might also approach other researchers for advice.

You should now have identified the two or three most likely prospects. Avoid the temptation to make an approach to all three at the same time in the hope that one might be successful. Few things are likely to irritate sponsors more than to find out that the application they have been processing so laboriously has also been put out for refereeing by another potential sponsor. Instead, select the sponsor that you feel is most likely to respond positively.

Conforming to the sponsor's requirements

Look very carefully at the sponsor's requirements. You will have ensured that your project falls within their terms of reference. Now you need to look at their administrative arrangements. Some organizations are prepared to receive applications at any time, others have fixed submission dates. Some simply ask for a letter of application (to which you should attach your carefully produced proposal), while others have formal application forms: some even limit the number of words you can use in different parts of the proposal.

Look out for any strings attached to the award. Some sponsors will not pay organizational overheads, others limit the overhead payments to a fixed proportion of salary costs. Some will automatically cover inflation increases and nationally agreed salary awards, others expect you to estimate the likely effect of these in advance. Some will meet the costs of research supervision, others expect the host organization to cover the salary of the research supervisor. Life is anything but straightforward.

Find out what is likely to happen to your proposal. It helps to know if it will go out to referees or if it will be considered by a standing committee or panel of advisers. To avoid the agonizing uncertainty, ask when you are likely to receive a decision on an application – few sponsors are able to turn applications around in much less than three months.

You then need to re-present your proposal so that it conforms to all the requirements of the sponsor. The last thing you want is for your proposal to be ruled out on technical grounds.

Informal discussions

If at all possible, try to discuss your ideas informally with the sponsor. Many are very good at this, particularly if you have not applied before, or if you are at the beginning of a research career.

Try to establish a dialogue, while recognizing that the person you are dealing with will have little spare time and many other things to do. Set out your ideas in outline first to establish that the subject of your research falls within the sponsor's terms of reference. Try to find out whether by making any modifications you could strengthen the proposal in the eyes of the sponsor – it may be, for example, that there are related issues in which the sponsor is interested, or which are best avoided.

If you can, see if the official you are dealing with will look at a draft of your proposal before finalizing it. Clearly they cannot offer a definitive opinion as the proposal will almost certainly have to go out to referees, but if you are going through the process for the first time, many officials will be prepared to let you have an informed view.

Remember to get the balance right. People working for research sponsors are generally very helpful and many of them are prepared to go to some trouble to help people who are making applications, particularly those who are doing it for the first time. But they are only human and they can become understandably irritated by the applicants who always seem to be ringing up to check this out, or to clarify that – particularly if they could have found the answer in the guidelines that they have already been sent. Make sure you do not step over the line.

View things from their perspective

When dealing with a sponsor, try always to look at the process from their point of view. The people with whom you will be dealing will almost certainly be interested in the subject of the research. But they may be more concerned with the need to allocate limited funds between a number of competing applications. They may be worried about spending their allocation during the financial year, or they may be even more worried because they have already over-committed their budget.

Subject to these constraints, they will be looking for research that is novel and innovative, that is likely to address high-priority needs and that is likely to be carried out in a competent and professional manner. They will want a high expectation that the research will produce a good, interesting report that will be widely circulated, arousing considerable interest and comment.

There is a tendency to avoid the contentious and the controversial although, equally, there is seldom support for projects that are bland and unlikely to make any ripples at all.

Making the submission

If you have done all of this, you will be in a good position to make your submission. You can adjust your proposal so that it fits with the sponsor's requirements and you can anticipate some, at least, of the questions that referees will ask. Double-check the addition, proof read it once again, make sure the application form is correctly completed with all the necessary signatures and then off it goes. Now begins the long wait.

When the decision is announced – assuming that it is positive – you should be prepared to make some amendments in the light of referees' comments. These are normally very sensible and worth taking on board. Do, however, be clear about any issues that are non-negotiable – there is little point in getting this far only to end up with a project that does not enable you to do what you wanted to do in the first place.

Sort out the administrative arrangements. Agree, for example, a starting date, check to see if the sponsor wants any involvement in the appointment of the research staff, find out what the arrangements are for claiming the grant, and so on. Then go out and celebrate.

If the decision is negative, it is always worth exploring whether it would be possible to submit an amended proposal to take account of referees' comments. This does not happen very often but you will have invested a great deal of effort to get this far and it is worth trying to keep the proposal alive. Ask, in as non-threatening a manner as you can muster, why the proposal was rejected. Make it clear that you are not trying to challenge the decision (even though it is clearly a daft one); rather, you are simply trying to understand where you went wrong so that you can avoid making the same mistakes twice. Consider asking a friendly researcher to look at the proposal and to give you a second opinion.

If, after all this, you still believe that you have got something that is worth funding, then begin the whole process over again with another funder.

Is it really worth it?

This question is often asked by people who have spent a long time preparing submissions, revising them, negotiating, renegotiating and resubmitting, only to be told that this year's funds have been allocated, but there is a good chance that next year . . . It is a question worth asking well before that stage is reached.

Research grants are time-consuming to obtain. There is considerable competition for limited funds and so you seldom stand better than a one-in-three or one-in-four chance of success. Becoming fully conversant with the procedures of even just one sponsor can be a lengthy process. It is clearly not worth the trouble unless you are applying for a fairly substantial amount of money.

Then there are the constraints that the award of external funds places on the research. The sponsor will have their own set of formal requirements that must be met. They might insist, for example, that you have an advisory committee, or that you produce quarterly reports on progress. They also have less explicit requirements. They might want you to highlight certain things that you do not recognize as important, or avoid issues that you want to explore. You could find yourself presenting the results in a moderated way to avoid controversy or the possibility that you will upset the sponsor.

On the other hand, external funds can do much to enhance the research. Clearly, they bring a level of resources that enables you to do more than otherwise would be possible. They also bring a seal of approval. The fact that a sponsor has seen fit to commit funds to your project gives it a status that it would not otherwise have. This can help you gain access to organizations and to get better response rates to surveys.

The funder might also help you gain access to a network of other researchers who are exploring related issues and could help you with your work. More generally, the sponsor will promote awareness of the research by publicizing it through their own channels.

Finally, the knowledge that a sponsor is looking over your shoulder will do much to encourage you to manage the project tightly and to deliver the results on time and within budget.

Responding to calls for tender

Responding to calls for tender requires a different approach, not least because the whole timescale becomes condensed. First we must distinguish between open and closed calls.

Open calls are the ones issued publicly by sponsors in which they advertise the fact that they are interested in receiving bids for a specified piece of work or for work in a somewhat wider area. The Directorates-General of the European Commission frequently issue such calls, indeed they are required to do so for all projects with budgets exceeding a certain limit. The topic of the research will be defined quite precisely in a lengthy specification and notice of the call will be posted on all the relevant Commission websites as well as being published in the *Official Journal*.

The Economic and Social Research Council also issues public open calls but these are rather different. They do not specify a particular project; instead they define a broad subject and invite proposals for research that falls within it.

Closed calls, on the other hand, are restricted to a much smaller number of organizations. Here, the sponsor first identifies the organizations that it thinks are capable of undertaking the work. They are then sent a detailed specification and invited to submit a proposal. Clearly, your chances of success in a closed call are greater than in an open one. For some of its open calls, the European Commission will receive more than 100 proposals, only one of which will be successful. The research councils receive a similar number out of which they may fund ten or a dozen projects. But in a closed call you may be bidding against only three or four competitors. The only problem is that you need to have a pretty strong track record before you get invited to bid.

It is becoming common for organizations that commission significant amounts of research to invite potential contractors to join what is usually known as a framework programme. Under this arrangement the contractors submit a statement of capabilities which sets out their experience, their track record of research, the skills and expertise of their staff and their terms of employment. These capability statements will be considered by the commissioning body, which will then invite the selected contractors to join the programme. Once you are in, the commissioning body will select potential contractors from the approved list whenever it wants to commission some research. The call for tenders will still be competitive, but the competition will be more limited.

The specification

The sponsor will have gone to some trouble to specify the work they want carried out. They usually provide some background to the work to put the project into context and to show how it has arisen. They then often identify a research aim and a set of objectives. Some also suggest the methods they expect contractors to use. You then have to respond by designing a study and, in some respects, turning the specification into a proposal.

The missing piece of information is usually the size of the budget. The sponsor will want to obtain the best possible value for their money and they will expect contractors to put in competitive bids. To encourage this, many will not say how much money is available. You have to make your best guess and hope that you are not advocating a £25,000 project to an organization that only has £10,000 to spend. Some of the more far-sighted sponsors do indicate what the budget ceiling is and this helps a great deal. They still get competitive bids – the difference is that people compete on quality and volume rather than on price.

If there is no indication of the size of the budget, and particularly if you suspect that your proposal is likely to require more money than you feel the sponsor has available, give them a ring and say that your preliminary thoughts suggest a project that will cost X thousand pounds, would this rule you out? If you hear a sharp intake of breath followed by a long silence, you can draw your own conclusions.

The specification should also clarify the submission procedure. With open calls it is quite common to have a two-stage process. The sponsor first invites potential applicants to submit an outline proposal indicating what they want to do. These are then used to select a short-list of applicants who are asked to submit full proposals. This saves time at both ends.

Pre-submission interviews

Many sponsors invite potential contractors to a meeting to discuss the bid before the proposals are submitted. This is your opportunity to clarify anything that is uncertain in the specification and to explore whether or not your interpretation is correct.

Meetings of this kind are really useful. You get a much better feeling for what it is that the sponsor wants and you can begin the process of establishing a working relationship with them.

The proposal

The proposal that you will submit in response to a call for tender is not very different from an unsolicited proposal to a responsive funder. It needs to demonstrate your competence, your understanding of the issues and your familiarity with the methods. You will need to take the aim and objective as given, although it is acceptable to qualify them slightly if you have spotted an ambiguity in the specification or if you feel that something has been missed out. You are on more shaky ground if you suggest that one or more of their objectives are superfluous and can be omitted.

The main area of difference lies in the fact that you have to sell yourself and your organization a little more vigorously. Remember that you will be competing with other individuals and organizations with backgrounds that are similar to yours. Your proposal should project a clear impression of what you have to offer that others do not. For this reason, many proposals that have been submitted in response to calls for tender begin with a section describing the organization and its potential.

As with all proposals, keep asking yourself what it is that the sponsor is looking for. Do they want novel and interesting research ideas around a general theme? If so, try to work out which angle they will be coming from; consider how the previous work they have funded will have led into the present call. Ask yourself how research under this call will fit with their other programmes. Try to look at other projects they have funded to get an idea of the scale and nature of the work they support – are they more interested in an academic approach or do they prefer projects with a very practical outcome?

If you are responding to a call for a specific project, keep returning to the specification, trying to get into the mind of the person who wrote it. Ask yourself how your proposal matches up to what they have asked for.

The selection interview

Few contracts are awarded on the basis of the proposal alone. In most cases you will be invited along to make a presentation and to answer questions about your proposal. Some potential contractors make a big thing of this. I once went to make a presentation where I followed one made by a large management consultancy fielding a team of 11 people complete with laptops, flipcharts and handouts. I felt quite overshadowed until I realized that they had all been crammed into a room that could comfortably hold only half the number. It is possible to go over the top.

The form of presentation you make is clearly a matter of personal preference. Some choose a low-key approach, taking the panel through the proposal and providing a little more detail on points that, with hindsight, might not be entirely clear. Others use it as an opportunity to promote their organization, and often themselves, and spend the time saying why they will be able to do the job better than others. Yet others use the opportunity to establish, or strengthen the basis of trust between them and the sponsor – projecting an image of honesty, reliability and competence.

Think about the thing analytically. First, the sponsor must have a degree of confidence in your ability to do the work. Either they would not have invited you to bid, or you would not have got onto the short-list. They have your proposal and so they know what you plan to do, and anyway there will be an opportunity in a few minutes time to quiz you on that. They know how much you are proposing to charge and have not ruled you out yet on that score. What the selection interview is designed to do is to enable them to find out whether they can work with you – whether they can trust you to do a good job.

In the light of this, the best approach seems to be to play things straight. Tell them a little about yourself and your organization, emphasizing your strong points and drawing their attention to aspects that they are unlikely to be aware of. Run through the proposal to refresh their memory, emphasizing the overall approach and explaining why you chose it. If you have varied from the specification in any way, explain the thinking that lay behind your decision to do so. And pretty much leave it at that. If you use audiovisual aids, make sure they work and that they can be set up easily. Few things irritate a selection panel more than having a potential contractor flapping around trying to connect the projector to their laptop and calling up the presentation. This is a real waste of the interview. Do not speak for more than your allotted time. Engage in lots of eye contact and smile as often as you can.

When the questioning begins, be honest and open. If you do not know the answer to a question do not try to waffle – it is only embarrassing. And keep on smiling. Try to sum them up. How will you feel working for them? Are they being sympathetic to your approach? Do they have a sense of humour? Are they smiling back?

Try not to get flustered. If there is more than one of you, make sure that everyone has a chance to speak (otherwise why are your colleagues there?). If you notice that there is someone on the panel who appears particularly sceptical, try to address your remarks to them and try to judge from their response how to overcome their scepticism. And keep smiling.

The importance of trust

Much of it is about establishing a working relationship based on trust. You have to trust the sponsor to deal with you responsibly. They have to trust you to carry out the work you are contracted to do to a level of quality that is acceptable and to deliver the results on time and within budget.

Throughout your dealings, you should be trying to build that relationship of trust. You might not win this contract but you do want to ensure you are asked to tender for the next one.

SUMMARY

External funding comes in two main forms depending on who has the idea for the research. Either you have an idea for a research project which you then take to a possible funder, or the funder announces that they want to commission a particular piece of research and you submit a proposal.

There are three main sources to which you can apply for research funds:

- research councils
- charities and foundations
- public sector bodies.

You can also approach companies for commercial sponsorship. One way to assemble funds for a big project is to create a consortium of funders. This is not, however, easy.

When approaching funders, the first thing to do is to make sure that you have identified the most appropriate source for your purpose. Decide on the type of funder and then work through the relevant directories and websites. Once you have selected the organization, study their requirements and, if possible, hold informal discussions to make sure that your proposal will fit in with their current priorities. Try to view things from their perspective and approach your dealings with them accordingly.

Responding to calls for tender is rather different. Some calls are publicly advertised and are open to anyone to apply, others are closed and limited to a small number of organizations which are invited to submit bids. Much depends on the specification issued by the sponsor. The proposal should emphasize the characteristics of you and your organization and should demonstrate why you will be able to do a particularly good job.

There will usually be a selection interview. You should use this to create a good impression and to begin to build a relationship of trust between you and the sponsor.

5

Manage the research

The big moment has arrived. After all your careful planning and preparation, you have received approval for the work or the funder has agreed to make the money available. Now you have to get the project on the road and, somehow, keep it going in the right direction.

The project plan

The first thing you should do is to turn the information that is contained in the proposal into a project plan – a document that will set out what you are going to have to do between now and the end of the research.

If you have a well worked-out proposal, this stage is not difficult. If you have been set a firm deadline by which time the project must be completed, then work backwards from this. You know how much time you planned to spend on different tasks, so you can now actually set dates for their start and completion. Now that you are working with actual dates, as distinct from notional weeks or months, you can begin to make allowances for things like public holidays – if your project runs over the winter, you will probably need, for example, to allow at least two weeks for the Christmas period.

If you do not have a fixed deadline, you can begin from now and work forward. You may not be able to start immediately. You may have to recruit staff, or to wait for them to finish work on other projects. It is, however, well worth fixing an actual start date as soon as you can and then to work towards it. Then pace things out from there. Remember to make allowance for things like the time needed to complete and return questionnaires. Check also that you are not committing yourself and the project staff to more days in a month than can be achieved.

Work out the critical path for the project, if you have not already done so for the proposal. This involves looking at each of the tasks and seeing whether they can be carried out concurrently or whether one needs to follow on from the other. This can be important if you are using sub-contractors – they will need to know when they can get started.

Identify milestones and deadlines for activities within the project. Make sure that everyone working on the study is aware of these and is prepared to work towards them. Prepare a detailed timetable and make sure that everyone associated with the project, including the sponsor, has a copy so that they know what is going on. Having everyone aware of the timetable like this is a very good way of forcing yourself to keep to it and to avoid slippage.

Staffing

If you are using staff who are already in post, make sure they can meet the requirements you have given them. They will need to be able to take holidays occasionally or they may have periods of training booked.

If you need to recruit staff, get the advertisements out as quickly as you can. Be reasonable in your expectations. You will probably be looking for someone who knows the subject, has appropriate research experience, is prepared to accept a limited-term contract, can start immediately and has a personality that will fit with yours. You may be lucky but you will probably have to compromise. Think things through and be clear about what it is that you are really looking for in a recruit. Identify the criteria that are essential and those that are merely desirable.

If the project is a short one, it will be difficult to recruit a researcher as few people are willing or able to consider jobs that only last for a month or so. In such cases explore the possibility of a secondment. Working on a research project is good for career development purposes and thus may be attractive to both employers and employees. It may also mean that you can attract someone who has practical experience that they can bring to bear. Even so, do not just accept anyone. Consider, in particular, their personality characteristics. If the work involves a lot of interviewing, then you need someone fairly extrovert and open. If it involves the management of a survey and the analysis of data then you will need someone who is very organized and systematic and who will pay attention to detail.

Finance

Give some thought to money when setting up the project. This may require nothing more than obtaining a code number on your organization's financial system. Alternatively, you may have to work closely with the finance department to make sure they understand what is happening, that they are prepared to issue invoices to the funder, and that they understand the basis on which the invoices are to be issued.

Critically, if an external funder is involved, make sure your finance people are aware that you will be incurring expenditure before you can claim it back. If they are not happy with this arrangement it is best to find out now, not, as happened to me once, when they stop paying your expenses, or worse, your salary.

Set up some kind of system that will enable you to keep track of expenditure. Staff costs will be the main item of expenditure and these are fairly constant and easy to monitor. Make sure you keep abreast of all other expenditure. A good finance department should be able to do this for you, but do not bank on it. You can do a great deal to track expenditure using a simple spreadsheet. And if you do, you will be in the secure position of always knowing where you stand in relation to your budget. You will be able to make savings where necessary before you actually run out of money.

Accommodation and support services

Far too many research workers have arrived at a new job to find that they do not have anywhere to sit. Make sure that you sort out accommodation and office services well in advance. The researchers will almost certainly need personal computers, telephone lines, stationery, access to photocopying facilities, library membership and so on.

If, as the project manager, you can anticipate these requirements and get everything ready before people arrive to start work you will hit the ground running. An organization I worked for always made sure that when staff arrived on their first day there was a pigeon-hole with their name on it, they were listed in the telephone directory and on their desk was an in-tray full of all the stationery they needed. These simple things created a positive view of the organization that took months to wear off.

You and the researchers will depend heavily on the organization's support services. Make sure that they have been warned about the project and that they know what to expect. Try to give them as much advance warning as possible of things like the printing of questionnaires.

Time spent sorting these things out in advance will be paid back with dividends later in the project.

Launching the project

You will quite possibly want to make a bit of a splash when the project begins. Not only will this help to give it some momentum from the outset, it can also help to alert the possible subjects of the research. It can also help to build a sense of identity and ownership among the project staff. In-house researchers will need to secure the support of their colleagues and to allay any fears that might otherwise develop.

Press releases

Issue a press release. Make it snappy and interesting. Focus on the problem that you will be studying and on the reasons why the research is important. Give an indication of what you will be doing and how long it will take to do it. And give a contact point for more information. Send this out to the appropriate media, checking first, of course, with your organization's press office. Send copies to the local paper, to any regional papers and to local radio and television stations as well as to the professional press. Use the press release as a means of notifying other organizations and individuals who you feel ought to be aware that the research is going on. Use this opportunity to begin building up a mailing list of people and organizations that are interested in the project.

Websites

Establish a website or a page on the organization's intranet. It need not be complicated but it will be useful for people wanting to track the project down. You should make an effort to keep it up to date, using it to publish discussion papers and interim findings.

Try to construct it so that people can register an interest, perhaps offering their own comments on the project.

Information sheets

It is also useful to produce a one- or two-page information sheet about the project. You will find numerous opportunities for sending these out over the coming weeks. The information sheet should expand on the press release, setting out the reasons for the research and indicating how you are going to go about it. It should include full contact details and might even invite people to register their interest in being kept informed of progress during the project.

Make a start

Sooner or later you are actually going to have to start the work. This is often much more difficult than it sounds and, strangely enough, it is one of the few things that become more difficult with each successive research project. Essentially, you have to build up sufficient momentum to carry you and your fellow researchers through the potentially difficult times to come. You have to get down to the library and start doing the literature search. Someone has to start compiling the mailing list for the postal questionnaire and so on.

Once you do get going, however, everything seems to take on a life of its own and you will wonder what all the fuss was about.

Monitoring progress

If something goes wrong in a research project, the linear nature of research – and the consequent lack of repetition – means that it is seldom possible to go back and do it again. This means that you have to monitor your progress, keeping on top of things, making corrections and overcoming problems as you go.

Meetings

From the outset, establish a pattern of regular meetings to review progress. At each of these, focus on what has been achieved and compare this with the project plan. If you are running ahead of schedule that is fine (and unusual) – just make sure you have not forgotten to do something. If you find the project slipping a little, search for ways in which you can catch up so that you reach your milestones on time.

Use the meetings to take stock of developments, discussing problems and the different ways of overcoming them. Continually look ahead to anticipate what is coming up and to prepare for it accordingly.

A sounding board

If you are working on the project alone, try to find someone who will act as a sounding board to enable you to discuss problems and issues as you go along and who can meet you periodically to review progress and to look out for those wretched milestones that keep coming up much more quickly than ever you expected. If all else fails, persuade your partner, parent, child or friend to listen to you. If you haven't got any of these, get yourself a cat.

Making up lost time

If things do begin to slip, try not to panic. If you have designed the project properly and have prepared a good project plan, you will have allowed for a little slippage and it is usually possible to make up lost ground. If it is more serious, then you might need to consider a range of options. First, can you push the deadline back? Think about the implications that this will have for the funder or for the person or organization that is waiting for the results of the research. Can you cut back on any of the later stages in the project? Think about the implications of this. If the later stages were seen as important when you wrote the proposal, how come you can scale them down now? Could you bring someone else in to take on some of the tasks and thus reduce the elapsed time required? If you do this, how will you finance it?

Whatever you decide to do, be quite open about it, especially if an external funder is involved. And once you have decided – do it.

Financial monitoring

As well as monitoring the progress of the work of the project, keep an eye on the budget. You will be able to forecast staff expenditure quite accurately, although there will always be the odd occasion when someone on the research team gets promoted and throws out your careful calculations. More particularly, monitor expenditure on travel and subsistence and on things like printing and postage. These are the difficult expenditure items to forecast in advance and you should make sure that you are unlikely to overspend.

Monitoring the results

Through your regular monitoring meetings, keep asking what you have learned so far. Keep trying to make sense of the results as they emerge. It may be that you will identify something that requires more detailed examination at a later stage in the project. Very occasionally you will come up with some early results which mean that you can cut out one of the later tasks. You will find that constantly thinking about the results as the work progresses will help enormously towards the end of the project as you try to make sense of it all. That being said, ensure that you keep an open mind. Do not jump to conclusions too soon because if you do you may find yourself interpreting later evidence selectively so that it supports your earlier conclusions.

Throughout all this, cling on to the aim and objectives of the project. Keep reminding yourself what it is that you are there to achieve. As they say, 'when you are up to your neck in mud and alligators, if is difficult to remember that you originally intended to clear the swamp.'

Discussion papers

To codify the results and to help clarify things in your own mind, it is often worth producing discussion papers during the project. Ask yourself what you have learned so far and try to get the results down on paper. These can be discussed with your colleagues, a supervisor or an advisory committee. It will help to keep them in the picture and it will help you to keep things focused.

Good communications are particularly important for in-house researchers. Many people can find research threatening. Their concerns may be unjustified but they are no less real. Be as open as possible and, whenever possible, share the information that you collect. A good friend, for example, was conducting participant observation in an elderly persons' care home. The other care staff found this threatening until she left a copy of the previous day's notes in the staffroom for anyone to look at.

The problem stages

There are a number of problem stages in all research projects. In part this is a personal thing – some people find some things more difficult than others but most researchers will have experienced some or all of these.

Getting started

As I mentioned above, this is something that I find gets progressively more difficult with each successive project. When you are doing your first half dozen pieces of research, your initial enthusiasm can help a great deal. Even so, it is difficult to make that very first step, beginning the process that will carry you forward to the end.

The trouble is that at the beginning of a project, there are so many other things that you can do to avoid starting the research. You can set up a filing system, make sure the finance department are on board, write a press release, use that nifty bit of software to start a mailing list, sharpen the pencils. Instead, you simply have to take a deep breath and get going.

Feeling lost halfway through

This is when you begin to become so absorbed in the complexity of the project that you start to lose track of why it is that you are doing the work. The survey has gone wrong, the reminder letters are stuck in the strike-bound sorting office, the computer has a virus and you despair of ever being able to understand SPSS. It seems to take so much of your energy and creative ability just to keep the project moving forward that any mention of results seems impossibly abstract and conceptually unattainable. It is at this point that you will be grateful for the statement of aim and objectives in the proposal. Cling on to it – things have a habit of sorting themselves out.

About this point you may also suffer the twin feelings of on the one hand knowing that you will never properly get to grips with the subject, it is far too complicated and would require a much more extensive project than yours, while at the same time feeling that it is all so trivial and self-evident that no-one in their right mind would go to the trouble of researching it. It is quite common to experience these two feelings at the same time. Do not despair. Keep plugging away and it will all come right in the end.

Being overwhelmed by data

This is a common characteristic of research projects with major survey components. The data can be qualitative or quantitative, there is no escape. The time comes when you stare at the pile of interview transcripts, or the stack of computer printout, and you wonder whether you will ever be able to make sense of it all.

Again, return to the proposal to make absolutely sure what it is that you are looking for. Get yourself, and the data, organized and work at it systematically. You can simply flick through the tables noting anything that looks interesting. Much better, though, to approach the data with particular questions in mind and a structured approach to the analysis.

Whatever you do, keep things well organized and documented.

Drawing things to a conclusion

The time will come when you need to call a halt and make sense of it all. There will always be a temptation to look further at this or that issue, to collect a little more data to verify your findings, or to talk to that person who you have just discovered is interested in the subject.

But you have to stop somewhere. A final deadline helps greatly. Part of the problem with drawing things to a conclusion is that this is what prefaces the hard slog of producing the report. You should recognize that your desire to look again at the analysis may only be your way of putting off the awful moment of starting to write the report.

Getting things down on paper

The final report is often the worst bit. Where to start? What to put in and what to leave out? How to cover the complexity? What am I actually trying to say? We will come to the process of writing the report later. Suffice it to say here that there is no substitute for working out what you are going to say and developing a detailed structure before you start writing. Once you have that detailed structure in front of you, your mind can concentrate on selecting the words, shaping them into sentences and deciding when it would be nice to start a new paragraph.

The next two chapters cover these issues in more detail.

Opposition from your colleagues

When working on a project inside an organization, it is not uncommon to come up against opposition from the organization's staff. This is a particular problem for in-house researchers. Good communications are the best way to overcome this. Make sure that everyone knows what the research is about, what the aim and objectives are and what methods you will be using. Make a special effort to contact the people who might be adversely affected by the results. You may not be able to reassure them but at least they will feel that you are not 'out to get them'.

Try to identify the main stakeholders. They are usually: the people who run the organization; the people who could be adversely affected; and the people who stand to benefit. Devise strategies that will enable you to communicate effectively with all of them.

Open up channels of communication early in the project, keep the channels open and make sure that everyone feels well informed. Work even harder to communicate the results of your research, and provide people with opportunities to discuss both the results and their implications.

Advisory and steering committees

Many experienced researchers try to avoid advisory and steering committees like the plague. They would rather work unsupervised without someone looking over their shoulder. They are usually making a mistake. Most of us benefit from a bit of advice and guidance every now and then. Advisory and steering committees can make a real contribution to the quality of the research.

First, though, it is important to be clear about the difference between the two types of committee. Advisory committees exist to support the researchers, offering comments and suggestions on the research methods and help with interpreting the results. The research staff, however, remain responsible for directing and managing the research. Steering committees, on the other hand, are there to steer the research project. They have a more formal rôle in directing the course of the research and, as such, they take ultimate responsibility for any decisions. Some of the problems that people have experienced, both as researchers and as committee members, stem from a fundamental confusion about these two rôles.

Making the most of the committee

As a researcher, the key to getting the most value out of a steering committee or an advisory committee lies in an attitude of mind as much as anything else. If you begin by thinking that the committee is an inconvenient nuisance, interrupting the research with its meetings and forcing you to do things you do not want to do – not least, adding to your workload by requiring you to produce reports and committee papers – then you are most likely to come to grief.

If, on the other hand, you approach the whole exercise more constructively, recognizing that the committee members do, in fact, have something valuable to contribute, then a supporting committee can do a great deal to improve the quality of the research. If you are in any doubt, ask someone who has served on such a committee.

Clearly, it is important that everyone involved understands whether the committee is to advise or to steer. To ensure this, it is often worth producing a set of terms of reference for the committee which you can send out to members when you invite them to join. Then, at the first meeting, return to it to make sure there is no ambiguity.

Select the members of the committee carefully and be clear in your own mind why each is being chosen. Some may be able to offer help with the research methods. Others can provide insights into the subject matter of the research, while others may be able to help you develop a good working relationship with the organizations that are the subject of your research.

If you are arranging either an advisory or a steering committee, it is normal to invite a representative of the funder to attend the meetings.

Once you have selected the members, work hard in the early days to ensure that they are engaged with the research. They will, probably, only have a hazy idea about the origins of the project and, with the best will in the world, you cannot expect them to do much more than quickly read the proposal. So, at the first meeting, make sure that you explain the background to the project and ensure that everyone is clear about the aim and objectives.

Managing the committee's work

Once the project – and the committee – is up and running, do all that you can to ensure that the committee operates effectively. In particular, try to make it as easy as possible for the members to participate. Begin by fixing a schedule of meetings. You will know what the research plan looks like so you can identify the critical points and the times when you will most benefit from the committee's support and advice. Book the meeting dates at the first meeting of the committee so that everyone knows when they will be expected to turn up. Try also to identify the purpose of each meeting – you might, for example, want a meeting to review the draft of a questionnaire; you will certainly want one to review a draft report. People will make a better contribution if they know what is expected of them.

Get the paperwork flowing smoothly. Each meeting should have a clear agenda and should be supported by written papers that people can look at in advance. Send the agenda and papers out at least a week before the meeting – two weeks is preferable. Have spare copies available at the meeting because there will always be someone who forgets to bring the papers with them.

Get the administrative arrangements right. If people are travelling from a distance, make sure that there is coffee available when they arrive. If the meeting starts or ends around lunchtime, either provide sandwiches or make some other arrangement so that people do not go hungry. Start and end the meeting on time – there is nothing worse than arriving on time, only to sit around waiting for the last person to turn up. Also, by ending at a pre-announced time you avoid that dismal type of end to a meeting where one by one the members slink out to get their trains.

It is normal to pay the expenses of people attending the meeting. When you send out the agenda for the meeting, always include a claim form that members can use and have spare copies available for those who forget to bring theirs to the meeting.

During the meeting, keep your contributions brief. If you are uncertain of your ground, there is a temptation to talk too much to avoid the possibility of others being too critical. Remember that you are there to listen and to learn. Remember also that the committee members will want the project to succeed – their names will be associated with it and they will not want it to fail. Think twice before you dismiss advice. Then think about it for a third time – people have been known to be right, even when at first you think they are wrong.

Encourage a lively debate and try to draw on the different types of expertise around the table. Try to make it fun.

Take full notes during the meeting and immediately afterwards produce a note listing all the action points. You will find this useful to refer to and if you send a copy to committee members the ones who attended will feel reassured that you took note of what was said, while those who could not make the meeting will be able to keep in touch with what is going on.

If anyone raises something contentious or clearly has a concern about the way the project is going and you are unable to satisfy that concern in the meeting, do not be afraid to contact them by telephone afterwards to discuss the issue in more detail.

At the end of the day, you have two choices: you can work with your committee, using them to raise the quality of the research; or you can fight against them, in which case you will all end the project feeling that it has been a waste of time.

Finally, remember to give the committee members a credit in the final report.

Living with your funder

The key to developing a successful relationship with your funder lies in understanding what it is that they want from the research. They will want to see a successful project that does credit to their organization. They want to spend the money they have set aside for the project, no more and no less, and they want to spend it during the agreed time period. Finally, they do not want any surprises.

Throughout the project, be open and communicative with your funder. Make sure they know exactly when the project is due to start and that you both share an understanding of when it is likely to finish. Check with them before you do anything publicly that might reflect on the funder. Do not, for example, issue a press release without first checking with them.

Try to build a working relationship with the person who is in charge of your grant or contract. They will almost certainly be the person who has been processing your application so they will already have some understanding of the background to the research, but telephone them to ask if there is any additional information that you can provide them with. Once the project has been going for a few weeks, invite them to visit. One possibility is to combine a visit with a meeting of the steering or advisory committee. They could arrive a couple of hours early and meet the other researchers.

Throughout the project, keep the funder's representative fully informed. Send them copies of discussion papers, draft reports, early results from the analysis, and so on. Put yourself in their place and ask yourself what information you would need to keep abreast of developments in the project. Remember that you are trying to avoid giving them any surprises.

If and when things go wrong, or the timetable begins to slip, do not try to conceal the fact from the funder. Much better to ring up and say that you are having a problem and that this is how you propose to overcome it. If the problem results in a change to the timetable or to some other fundamental aspect of the project, discuss it with the funder and follow up the discussion with a written note just to cover the possibility of a change in responsibilities within the funding body – then whoever takes over the project will have a documented file showing everything that is going on.

As the project comes to its end, keep the funder well informed about the probable conclusions and recommendations. This is particularly important if the results are likely to be contentious. Very few funders would ever try to suppress a controversial finding, although some may advise you to tone things down. The overwhelming majority will back you providing that you have given them prior warning. The last thing they want is a journalist ringing up out of the blue asking them to comment on something of which they are unaware.

At this stage in the project you will also be discussing dissemination with them. They may want to publish the report and most funders can do a great deal to help raise awareness of the research results. Remember to give them full credit in any report or article that is published.

Delivering the report on time will endear you to a sponsor. Far too many research reports are delivered late. Deadlines are missed and promises are broken. Try to avoid this at all costs.

Then, when the project is finished, the report published and all the fuss has died down, try to maintain some form of contact with the funder. If the report is reviewed, send them a copy of the review. If some kind of action is taken as a result of the recommendations, tell them. Who knows when you might have to call on them again?

SUMMARY

The first thing to do is to turn the information contained in the proposal into a project plan. This will set out all the things you need to do between the start and finish of the project, noting the milestones and deadlines. In most cases you do this by working backwards from the final deadline.

Recruit the research staff or, if they are already in post, make sure that they have time available when you need them. Establish the financial procedures, working closely in partnership with the finance department of your organization. Make sure that office accommodation, stationery and other equipment is ready and waiting for the research to begin. And ensure that the organization's support services know what is going on.

Launch the project and do it with a splash to help build up the momentum. Issue a press release, establish a website, compile information sheets about the project. Above all, start the work.

Once the project is up and running, monitor progress frequently and regularly. Hold regular meetings to review progress, trying to identify problems as they emerge and before they become really serious. If, despite this, things do go wrong, try to identify ways in which you can put the project back on track.

Monitor expenditure against your budget. And, as the results begin to come in, look at them carefully, trying to build up a picture of what is happening.

Be aware of the problem stages in a project and recognize them for what they are – things that everyone experiences.

Make the most of advisory and steering committees. Regard them as a support rather than a burden. Select the members carefully and work hard to make it possible for them to participate. Pay attention to what they say, especially if it contradicts your own views.

Develop a good working relationship with your funder. Remember that they want to see a project that will do credit to their organization, a steady and predictable expenditure of money and no surprises. Keep the funder well informed at all stages, especially as the project draws to a close.

6
Draw conclusions and make recommendations

This is the point everything has been leading up to. Having carried out the research and marshalled all the evidence, you are now faced with the problem of making sense of it all. Here you need to distinguish clearly between three different things: results, conclusions and recommendations.

Results are what you have found through the research. They are more than just the raw data that you have collected. They are the processed findings of the work – what you have been analysing and striving to understand. In total, the results form the picture that you have uncovered through your research. Results are neutral. They clearly depend on the nature of the questions asked but, given a particular set of questions, the results should not be contentious – there should be no debate about whether or not 63 per cent of respondents said 'yes' to question 16.

When you consider the results you can draw conclusions based on them. These are less neutral as you are putting your interpretation on the results and thus introducing a degree of subjectivity. Some research is simply descriptive – the final report merely presents the results. In most cases, though, you will want to interpret them, saying what they mean for you – drawing conclusions.

These conclusions might arise from a comparison between your results and the findings of other studies. They will, almost certainly, be developed with reference to the aim and objectives of the research. While there will be no debate over the results, the conclusions could well be contentious. Someone else might interpret the results differently, arriving at different conclusions. For this reason you need to support your conclusions with structured, logical reasoning.

Having drawn your conclusions you can then make recommendations. These should flow from your conclusions. They are suggestions about action that might be taken by people or organizations in the light of the conclusions that you have drawn from the results of the research. Like the conclusions, the recommendations may be open to debate. You may feel that, on the basis of your conclusions, the organization you have been studying should do this, that or the other. Another person my feel that your conclusions suggest that the organization needs to do something slightly different. So, again, recommendations need to be supported by structured and logical arguments.

These three concepts – results, conclusions and recommendations – are closely related but quite distinct from each other. Considerable confusion can arise if the report fails to make the distinction clear.

Analyse and synthesize the results

Part 2 of this book describes the procedures that can be used when you are analysing data. Here we will assume that the initial analysis has been completed and that you are now facing sets of tables and grids of information presenting the results of interviews and discussion groups. Your job now is to convert the data into information.

The first thing you must do is to get things organized. Make sure that you have easy access to all the data that you need and that all the results have been collected in and processed. In some projects it may not be sensible to wait until all the data is collected before beginning to analyse it. It will be better to undertake the analysis and synthesis as you go along, building up a composite picture. The only problem with this approach is that the early results tend to condition the way you look at the material that becomes available later, introducing a bias.

Check for accuracy and validity

Check that the preliminary analysis has been carried out satisfactorily. Look for any underlying errors or unexpected results. If appropriate, check that the usual tests of statistical significance have been carried out. Look at response rates and decide whether or not to use the data. I once reviewed a research report which began by saying that the 16 per cent response rate meant that it was necessary to treat the results with extreme caution. There followed 45 pages of report which appeared to treat the results as if they were utterly reliable.

Check whether statistics have been rounded up or down, check that the percentages make sense – do they refer to the rows or to the columns? Check that data are comparable, that the statistics have been collected over comparable time periods. Where appropriate, remember to make allowance for any differences when interpreting the results.

A map of the results

If the project is small, it is possible to absorb and retain most of the information and to think through the implications of the results you have found, arranging and re-arranging the data and information in your mind until it makes sense. This is just not possible in larger projects and here you must try to build up a mental map of the data – what is covered by this survey, how we dealt with various issues? – so that you can retrieve the necessary data when you need it. Many people find it useful to spread everything out over the floor at this point.

Make sure that you are clear about the results of the different stages of the work and the results that have been derived from the different methods. They will tell you different things and will need to be treated in different ways – the fact that 60 ~~~~~~~~~~~~~~ questionnaire respondents felt positively about some~~~~~~~~~~~~~~~~~~~~~~~~~~~~ fact that six out of the ten p~~~~~~~~~~~~~~~~~~~~~~~~~~~~ similarly positive. You use dif~~~~~~~~~~~~~~~~~~~~~~~~~~~~~ u should treat the results diff~~~~~~~~~~~~~~~~~~~~~~~~~~~~~~

Conclusions

TIP

* Any errors
* Unexpected results
* Make room for differences.
* Each section makes sense
* each result is treated differently.

Randor~

You coul~~~~~~~~~~~~~~~~~~~~~~~~ ies and exceptions, for trend~~~~~~~~~~~~~~~~~~~~~~~ ysis in this way. But this is a~~~~~~~~~~~~~~~~~~~~~~~ and it is very time-consumi~~~~~~~~~~~~~~~~~~~~~~~ later revealed to be importa~~~~~~~~~~~~~~~~~~~~~~~

It is ~~~~~~~~~~~~~~~~~~~~~~~ to what will now be a pretty~~~~~~~~~~~~~~~~~~~~ in what it is that you are loo~~~~~~~~~~~~~~~~~~~~~ g to answer and why were they important. ~~~~~~~~~~~~~~~~~ work that you can use to approach the data. Try to imagine the results that you would expect to see – the things that would support your hypothesis if you have one, or the things that would confirm your general expectations if you do not. Try also to imagine what would run counter to your expectations.

With this analytical framework in mind, approach your data. Not in a random way, but looking at different sources of data according to the issue that you want to clarify.

Work steadily and methodically, checking for patterns and trends and looking for inconsistencies. Keep focused on the research objectives, asking yourself what this piece of evidence tells you – what do you deduce from the fact that there is a consistent pattern, or what does the fact that this group is very different from the rest tell you? Above all, try to *understand* what the data is telling you, rather than simply processing it.

As you begin to structure your evidence within your analytical framework, look for other evidence that will support or refute your early analysis. Try to keep an open mind. It is always tempting to select evidence that supports an early view and to discount data that undermines it. But this is what it is all about – you are not there to reinforce your prejudices.

Avoid the traps

Avoid the obvious traps. First of all, avoid non-existent causal relationships. When two things that could be related demonstrate similar trends or patterns there is a temptation to assume that one thing causes the other. This may be the case but you will need to use other evidence to prove or disprove it. One researcher, for example, has shown that, since the late 1940s, there has been a nearly identical growth in the rise of juvenile delinquency and the use of ball-point pens. The two trends are unlikely to be linked by any causal relationship, although both might be products of the rise of a consumer society.

Even where events are related, the nature of the relationship may be obscure. A change in one variable is seldom caused solely by changes in one other. More commonly, there are several variables that together cause changes and, in looking at the relationships between single variables, the true picture is obscured. In such cases, look at things in the round – try to consider all the different facets before coming to a conclusion.

In other cases the process of aggregation can hide things of significance. This is often the case with statistical information containing proportions and percentages. A case in point occurred some years ago when, despite a high general rate of inflation, it appeared that the average price of books was falling. This surprised many people buying books for libraries as they felt they were experiencing high inflation rates all round. Table 6.1 shows what was happening:

Table 6.1 *The average price of books*

Category of book	Year 1		Year 2		Change (%)	
	Average price	Number published	Average price	Number published	Average price	Number published
Fiction	£8.00	500	£9.00	800	+12.5%	+60.0%
Children's	£4.00	400	£4.50	550	+12.5%	+37.5%
Non-fiction	£16.00	1000	£18.00	750	+12.5%	−25.0%
Total	£11.36	1900	£11.04	2100	− 2.8%	+10.5%

The average price of each category of book was increasing, but the drop in the overall average price can be explained by the change in the proportions of the different types of books published in the two years.

So, be careful when using aggregated data and wherever you can check what the disaggregated figures look like.

When analysing the results of interviews or questionnaire surveys, make allowances for different life-experiences. Someone in a rural area is likely to have a different perspective on public transport from someone living in central London. Equally someone born in the first quarter of the 20th century will have had a very different experience of life from that of someone born in the last quarter. Their experiences are likely to colour their judgments and their responses to your questions.

Above all, avoid the trap of making more of the results than is justified by the evidence. If the evidence is slender, do not try to strengthen it artificially. Present it for what it is, especially if you are unable to find any supporting evidence from your research.

Finally, having sifted all your results, consider whether additional data would be useful. It may not be possible for you to collect the data but it may be worth recommending that it be collected in future.

Draw your conclusions

Start from each of your research objectives. For each, ask yourself whether, on the basis of the evidence you have analysed, it is reasonable to conclude that . . . If your answer is 'yes' then you need to be able to present the argument or the logical statement that enables you to move from finding to conclusion. If the answer is 'no' then you will need to put forward a qualified conclusion.

Many people are tentative about advancing conclusions. Doing so means putting yourself on the line and, as a consequence, opening yourself up to challenge. This is understandably threatening. Remember, however, that by this time you have been looking in depth at the issue and, quite possibly, you know more about it than anyone else. If you cannot arrive at a conclusion now, then when will you ever be able to do so?

Set out all your conclusions with their supporting evidence and then play devil's advocate. Try to prove yourself wrong. Ask if there is any alternative interpretation that can be put on the results. Pick someone whom you know to have views that contradict your own and ask yourself how they would view things. Would they come to the same conclusions? If not, how would they interpret the results? Are their conclusions as valid as yours?

Look for overall consistency within your report. Check that each conclusion is supported by the others, not contradicted by them. Look carefully at the drafting to make sure there is no room for ambiguity or differences in the ways in which the conclusions will be read.

Make recommendations

Recommendations are suggestions to someone to do something. The recommendations should flow logically from the conclusions of the research and they should be carefully drafted to ensure that the right person or body takes the right action about the right thing.

Wherever possible, recommendations should be precise. Detail is seldom necessary, precision always so. Precision, however, needs to correspond with the target of the recommendation and the certainty with which you put it forward. If you are not able to specify precisely who should do something, or if you are a little tentative about what should be done, then it would be pointless to be very precise.

Let us suppose that you have conducted a piece of research into the association between training and motivation in an organization and one of your conclusions was that the design of effective training programmes was impaired by a lack of information about skills and training needs. This could give rise to a general recommendation such as:

Information about skills and training needs should be improved.

This covers the point but is rather vague and it could easily become lost or forgotten. It could be sharpened considerably by directing it at whoever was going to be responsible for taking the action:

The personnel department should improve the collection of information about skills and training needs.

This targets the recommendation and makes it less easy for someone to avoid it. But it does not indicate why the information needs to be improved. To do this it might be worth adding another phrase:

The personnel department should improve the collection of information about skills and training needs in order to assist the development of training programmes.

Even this does not really indicate the ways in which the present information is deficient and in need of improvement. If the personnel department is unlikely to work this out for themselves, it would be worth extending the recommendation to read:

> The personnel department should, within the next three months, improve the collection of information about the skills currently possessed by individuals and their individual training needs as identified through the staff appraisal process in order to assist the development of training programmes.

This makes things much more specific and allows little room for escape by the personnel department. It even sets a deadline for the work. This may not be tactically appropriate, in which case abandon the specificity and include something that calls for action while implying a degree of accountability:

> The personnel department should review the collection of human resource data about skills and training needs in order to assist the development of training programmes.

Note the use of the term 'human resource data' – getting the terminology right can be half the battle.

It is all a question of aiming the recommendations in the right direction and expressing them in the most appropriate format. Always try to look at the recommendations from the point of view of the person at whom they are targeted – and if you think they would antagonize them, then redraft accordingly.

SUMMARY

It is important to distinguish between results, conclusions and recommendations:

- Results are what you have found through the research. They are the processed findings of the work.
- Conclusions are less neutral than results. They are your interpretation of the results and are thus more subjective.
- Recommendations are suggestions about action that might be taken by people or organizations in the light of the conclusions that you have drawn from the results of the research.

First check the accuracy and validity of the results. Structure your analysis by returning to the research objectives and constructing an analytical framework, building up lists of questions that you want to answer and evidence that you will be looking for. Work steadily and methodically, trying to understand, rather than simply process the data.

Avoid analytical traps. Beware of apparent causal relationships. Be careful when using aggregated data. Allow for people's different life-experiences.

Draw conclusions from the evidence before you. Ask yourself if it is reasonable to conclude that . . . Check the evidence and try to validate your conclusions. Play devil's advocate and challenge yourself. Try to defend your conclusions with structured and logical arguments.

From your conclusions, make recommendations. Target the recommendations specifically and make them as precise as you can. Drafting is very important, and consider each recommendation from the perspective of the person to whom it is directed.

7

Write the report

No research project is complete without some form of report. Without a report, the only people to benefit from the work are the researchers.

The nature of the report should be determined by the project itself and by the audience to which the report is addressed. Short projects carried out within an organization may simply be reported by means of a brief paper supported by an oral presentation. Academic research, on the other hand, is expected to result in lengthy dissertations which cover all aspects of the research and report on them in a rather formal, predetermined way. Between these two extremes there is considerable scope for variety.

Structure

Most reports, no matter what their size or formality, follow a common basic structure. You must say why the work was done, what events led up to it and what other work was relevant. You must state the aim and objectives and describe what you did in order to achieve the objectives. This leads you through to the results, the conclusions you draw from the results and then to the recommendations.

These elements represent a common basic framework that you can start with when planning the structure of your report. You will almost certainly have to deviate in some way from the basic structure but it will provide you with a starting point.

Building up an outline

The trick about writing good reports is to think things through in advance and to build up a structured outline before beginning the actual process of writing. Before you start writing the first paragraph you should know how many chapters the report will contain, what will be the main and subheadings within each chapter and what material will be put in appendices. You should know roughly how long the report will be and what it will look like at the end of the day. You should also have a very clear idea of the audience for which you are writing.

You should ask yourself what sort of people they are, what prior knowledge of the subject they will bring to the report, how long they are likely to spend looking at it and who they might pass the report on to.

Begin by thinking about the nature of the research and the expectations of the audience. This will tell you whether the report is to be big or small, formal or informal, focused on methods and their application or on results and recommendations.

Chapters

Then decide on the basic structure. How many chapters will you have and what will they contain? You will need an introductory chapter at the beginning and something for conclusions and recommendations at the end. Work out what needs to come between. Think about the flow of material and the need to build up an understanding in people's minds. Most pieces of writing work best when they move from the general to the specific, so put the background and contextual material before your results. In most cases the overall structure at chapter level suggests itself. Something that is not always self-evident is whether to put the description of the methods you used in an appendix or to leave them in one of the early chapters: ask yourself what your audience would expect or would find most useful. These days I find it best to describe the methods briefly towards the beginning of the report, but also to have an appendix which contains a full discussion of what went on.

Main and subheadings

Once you have decided on the chapters, think through the structure of each in turn. What are you going to say first, what comes next and how will you wind it all up? Think of the main headings within the chapters. Once you have got these in place, think through what comes under each main heading. Work out the order in which you are going to present the information. Try to think of it in a linear way because that is how it will appear to the reader – one concept following another.

This kind of thing gets much easier the more times you do it. If you feel that you are stuck and cannot for the life of you see what the structure should be, it is possible that you have simply got too many things floating around in your mind, jostling for prominence and trying to ensure that they will not be forgotten. Try taking a fresh piece of paper and simply noting down all the concepts or issues that you think are relevant to that chapter or that section of a chapter. Write them down randomly on the page. This fixes them and seems to free up brain capacity to think about structure rather than simply trying to remember everything that needs to go in.

Then look at the sheet of paper and try to spot links between the things you have written down. If you begin with this, where will that issue come? How can you relate this to that?

Think about levels within the structure. Some concepts are of equal weight or importance; some are subordinate to others. Reflect these relationships in your structure. You will find that a sequence begins to suggest itself. At the very least, you will be able to identify clusters of issues that fit together. Keep working at it until you can fit all the things you listed into a single sequence. Figure 7.1 shows the structure I developed when planning this chapter.

Keep working at the structure, adding detail and putting things in the right place until you feel confident that you have covered everything. Do not worry about spending too much time on this stage of writing the report. Each hour spent working out a detailed outline will save you at least two hours of writing time later and will enable you to produce a much more balanced and logical report at the end of the day.

Length

Once you have the outline, think about length. How long does your report have to be? Students are often given a limit for the number of words their dissertations can contain. If you are not in that position, you have to work out whether you are going to produce a report with 20, 50 or 100 pages. What will your audience expect? Once you have decided, convert pages to word length (most typescript contains between 400 and 500 words on a page) and begin to allocate words to chapters and then to the main headings. This will give you a guide to write to and will help to avoid the tendency to use half the words in the first two chapters and then to squeeze the remaining five chapters into the space that remains.

You are now ready to begin writing.

The introduction

The first section of the report is the introduction. This provides the general background to the work. It should set the context within which everything that follows needs to be considered. It should provide a brief historical introduction, bringing in other relevant research or development work. This will lead you on to the justification for your study, the specific events that brought it about or the nature of the problem that precipitated it.

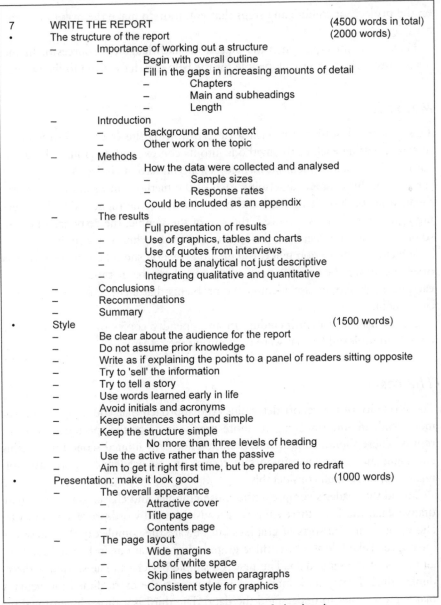

7	WRITE THE REPORT		(4500 words in total)
•	The structure of the report		(2000 words)
	–	Importance of working out a structure	
		– Begin with overall outline	
		– Fill in the gaps in increasing amounts of detail	
		– Chapters	
		– Main and subheadings	
		– Length	
	–	Introduction	
		– Background and context	
		– Other work on the topic	
	–	Methods	
		– How the data were collected and analysed	
		– Sample sizes	
		– Response rates	
		– Could be included as an appendix	
	–	The results	
		– Full presentation of results	
		– Use of graphics, tables and charts	
		– Use of quotes from interviews	
		– Should be analytical not just descriptive	
		– Integrating qualitative and quantitative	
	–	Conclusions	
	–	Recommendations	
	–	Summary	
•	Style		(1500 words)
	–	Be clear about the audience for the report	
	–	Do not assume prior knowledge	
	–	Write as if explaining the points to a panel of readers sitting opposite	
	–	Try to 'sell' the information	
	–	Try to tell a story	
	–	Use words learned early in life	
	–	Avoid initials and acronyms	
	–	Keep sentences short and simple	
	–	Keep the structure simple	
		– No more than three levels of heading	
	–	Use the active rather than the passive	
	–	Aim to get it right first time, but be prepared to redraft	
•	Presentation: make it look good		(1000 words)
	–	The overall appearance	
		– Attractive cover	
		– Title page	
		– Contents page	
	–	The page layout	
		– Wide margins	
		– Lots of white space	
		– Skip lines between paragraphs	
		– Consistent style for graphics	

Figure 7.1 *The structure for this chapter of the book*

The introduction should then set out the purpose of the research, specifying the aim and objectives and listing any hypotheses that you were trying to test. It is often useful to comment on any limitations or constraints that were placed on the project, or to note any steps that you took to make the task more manageable.

Finally, the introduction is the place to acknowledge the sources of finance for the research and to thank people for the help they have given to the work.

Methods

This section should begin with a description of the overall design of the research, putting each of the methods into its context and describing the different functions each of them performed. Then you have a choice. You can either carry on in this chapter, describing each of the methods in turn, how you used them, what the problems were and how you overcame them and, for surveys, noting the populations surveyed, the size of the sample, the response rates and so on. Or you can relegate all this information to a technical appendix.

Whichever choice you make, the methods section should cover the sequence of events during the research project, showing how the methods complemented each other. It should also identify the problems that arose and how you overcame them.

It may also be worth including in an appendix copies of forms, questionnaires and topic guides that were used during the research.

The results

The formality of the report determines the approach that you adopt here. The more academic the research, the more precise must be the specification of the results. There should be little interpretation and only limited scope for selecting and highlighting the most important results. In less academic reports, the formality can be relaxed considerably.

To aid the reader's comprehension, use graphics and charts to present quantitative data. But keep these simple. Spreadsheets and word-processing software allow you to use all sorts of graphics but beware the complexity that these can introduce. Take a look at the three graphical presentations in Figure 7.2. They all represent the same data. The first is a simple bar chart. The second is three-dimensional. It may look more exciting but does the extra dimension actually make it any easier to understand the data? The third is a three-dimensional pie chart. Again, it is technically more sophisticated, but does this make it easier to understand? Added sophistication is not always desirable.

When presenting the results of qualitative research, use quotations from interviews to illustrate the points that you are making. When used well, these

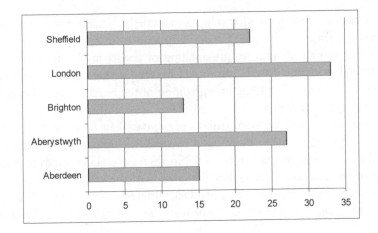

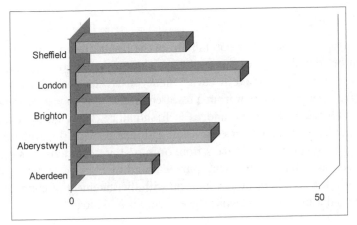

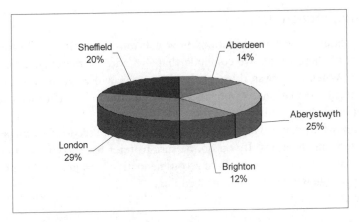

Figure 7.2 *Simple and complex graphics*

quotations will give life to what might otherwise be a fairly dry report. But do not overdo them.

While a straight descriptive presentation of results my be appropriate in a very formal academic dissertation, it can be very boring. In most reports, the readers will be expecting some interpretation of the results – some kind of discussion to make sense of it all.

Here you can draw on your analysis of the data, emphasizing the significant findings and beginning to build up a reasoned argument. In such cases you should try to integrate the results produced from different methods or different stages of the research. Remember that you used the different approaches to complement each other and to introduce different perspectives on an issue. Now is the time to integrate these to provide the readers with the full picture.

Conclusions

The conclusions should flow naturally from the results. Indeed, in some reports it might be sensible to have the results, conclusions and recommendations in a single chapter. Try to make it clear when you are presenting a conclusion. Remember that it is different from a research result – it is your interpretation or deduction based on the results and, as such, should be clearly identifiable.

It often helps to state your conclusion and then provide the evidence or the argument to support it. In conversation, or in oral presentations, it is more natural to set out a line of argument, pursue it and then arrive at the conclusion. This works less well in print. If you begin with the statement or conclusion people can hold it in their mind while the evidence is presented.

Recommendations

In most cases the recommendations flow naturally from the conclusions – 'in the light of these results we conclude that . . . and we therefore recommend that . . .' When writing in this way, however, you will want to draw attention to the recommendations. So put them in bold type or in italics to give them the emphasis they require.

You may find that it will be useful to have a separate section in which you list all the recommendations. If you do, be sure to refer back to the section of the report that gives rise to each of the recommendations; otherwise there is a danger that people will read them out of context.

Summary

There will also be people who will not have enough time to read your whole report. For them you need to provide a summary. Even those who do intend to read the report in full will benefit from looking at the summary first – it will give them an overall picture that they can use to put each element within the report into its proper context.

The summary may simply be the list of recommendations. You will make greater impact, however, if you summarize each chapter, listing the key points so that in two or three pages you have a précis of the full report. At the time this will seem very tedious, particularly as it is a task that you come to at the end of the writing process and you will be feeling rather tired and jaded. So make the chapter summaries as you go along. This helps to focus your mind and you will be very glad when you get to the final chapter and the summary is already written for you.

You will be able to adapt the summary for other purposes. You might produce a free-standing fact sheet on the research, you could mount it on your website, you could use it as the basis for a journal article. A good summary can be used over and over again.

A similar approach is needed for references and the bibliography. Compile these as you go along. Never refer to a publication when you are writing without adding the full citation to the bibliography. Again, you will be eternally grateful when you get to the end of the report and you know that you do not have to dig out all those obscure publications (some of which will have been returned to the library by then, you can be sure) and fiddle with the precise form of citation.

Writing in style

When asked about style, Matthew Arnold is reputed to have said: 'People think I can teach them style. What stuff it is. Have something to say and say it as clearly as you can. That is the only secret of style.' He has a point, but not everyone finds that it comes naturally. It does, however, get easier if you follow a number of fairly simple guidelines.

Be clear about your audience

Work out who you are writing for. Think about the time they will be able to devote to the report and the circumstances in which they will be reading it. Ask yourself what they will want to get out of reading the report, what they will do as a result.

You may not be writing for a single audience, in which case you have a problem. You can try to arrive at a compromise but it is probably better to write for one group and then also produce another summary or a set of key findings that are directed at the other group.

Do not assume prior knowledge

Remember when you are writing the report that you have just spent as much time as anyone studying the subject. You must not assume that all your readers will be as familiar with the topic as you are. Keep explanations simple and avoid the use of jargon.

A panel of readers

When you get stuck for a phrase or a sentence, imagine that you have a small panel of readers sitting across from your desk. Ask yourself what you would say to them. Put things in words and say them out loud to see how they flow.

Try to avoid being too formal, but at the same time do not patronize your readers. If something is complex, try to imagine the sort of questions they would ask.

Sell the information

You are trying to get a message over. Try to communicate it in the most effective way. Make it sound interesting. Again, think of the people sitting across the desk. Ask yourself what would convince them, what would be the issues that would most attract and hold their attention.

If you are writing for a diverse audience, try to make the report come alive from the first chapter. Stuff all the boring bits about response rates away in an appendix and begin with a vivid account of why it is that the research was so important. Be simple and direct and focus on the important bits.

Try to tell a story

This is the difference between producing a descriptive account of the results, and synthesizing and integrating them into a seamless whole that sheds light on the issues. Ask yourself what is the story that the results are trying to tell you – what does it all add up to? Work hard to make the whole greater than the sum of the parts.

Use words learned early in life

You will gain very little by using complex, sophisticated language. When you have a choice between two words with the same meaning, choose the simplest – this usually means the words that we learned first in life. So, avoid words like 'erroneous', 'endeavour' or 'terminate'. In their place use 'wrong', 'try' and 'end'. This will make your report easier for everyone to read. In particular, it will help people whose first language is not English.

The possible exception to this comes when you are writing academic dissertations. A particular style of writing has developed among academics and you will need to copy – sorry, emulate – it. In this style, complex words, and convoluted sentence constructions are quite acceptable; indeed, they often seem to be required by the readers.

To pick up the style, read a few academic papers in scholarly journals in your field and be guided by them. Once you have completed your dissertation, be prepared to shift back to plain English again as soon as you can, if you are planning to write for non-academic audiences.

AIA – Avoid initials and acronyms

The use of initials and acronyms is the worst form of arrogance. People use them because they save their own time, when speaking or writing. They do not save the time of the person listening or reading. In fact, there is quite a lot of research evidence to show that, when reading, it takes more time to decode a string of initials than it does to read the phrase when it is spelled out in full. And that applies when the initials or the acronyms are known to the reader. When they are not, the flow of the text is abruptly halted as the reader searches back through previous pages to find the first mention of the initials or, just as bad, has to search in a glossary.

When you use a set of initials instead of spelling something out in full, you are, in effect, saying to the reader, 'I know it is inconvenient for you, but it saves a little of my time so, I'm sorry, you will just have to put up with it.'

The only exceptions are the very commonly accepted acronyms like NATO or UNICEF, or initial-strings like the IMF or the EU. Even these, however, are specific to a cultural context. A development worker in a rural community in Asia will probably know what the IMF and UNICEF are but they will not necessarily know what NATO or the EU stands for. So beware: if there is any doubt, spell it out in full every time.

Keep sentences short and simple

On the whole, short sentences are more easily understood than long ones. And simple sentences are easier to understand than complex ones. So, avoid sentences that continue for line after line. Aim for an average sentence length of 20 words or less. Your word-processing software will almost certainly be able to tell you what your average is. (The average sentence length for this chapter, so far, is 16 words.)

Avoid the complexity that comes with more than one subclause within a sentence. If you find that you are having to introduce a number of qualifying statements into a sentence, try to restructure things so that you convey the same information in a number of shorter sentences.

Avoid artificially shortening sentences by missing out key words like 'a', 'the' and 'that'. It may give you a shorter sentence but it may also introduce ambiguity. Consider this brief, but somewhat confusing, statement found in a public library:

> Books for lending around the walls, those for reference on island bookcases.

Take care with your punctuation. Use it to signal changes within sentences. If you are not sure of the basics of grammar, then it is well worth taking the opportunity to refresh your memory of the underlying principles.

Keep the structure simple

This takes us back to your report outline. This should set out quite clearly the structure of the information within each chapter. From it you should be able to identify the main headings and, within these, the subheadings that will be used to label the information you present. You thus have two levels of headings: main headings and subheadings.

Before you start writing, decide how you will present these in the report. You might decide to use bold capitals for the main headings with a line space above and below. While for subheadings you could use bold italics with a line space above but none below. Apply these typographical devices consistently as you write the report and you will save yourself having to do another irksome task when you finish.

Most clearly structured writing can manage with two levels of heading. In some cases it might be necessary to introduce a third but this is rare.

Use the active voice rather than the passive

Much academic writing uses the passive voice – 'the data were analysed to show the characteristics of the population sampled.' This tends to be rather stilted and less than easy to understand. The same concept can be made more accessible by using the active voice – 'we analysed the data to show the characteristics of the population that we sampled.'

Aim to get it right first time

It is always worth aiming to produce the final draft on the first attempt. To write in the knowledge that you will redraft encourages carelessness. All too often, the draft that results requires major work, sometimes complete restructuring. Better to aim for perfection first time. Sometimes you achieve it and even when you do not, all that is required is minor amendment.

Word-processors are a mixed blessing here. Because they make it so easy to move text around there is a tendency to think that the important thing is to get the ideas down – we can structure them later. This is generally fatal. It is true that you can easily amend word-processed text, but you cannot easily impose a structure after the event – you simply end up with a disjointed and unbalanced set of paragraphs rather than text which flows sequentially and that has a logic and a rhythm to it.

Presentation

After you have put all that effort into writing the report, you deserve a report that looks good. Not only will this make you feel more positive about the report, good presentation will go a long way towards increasing its impact.

The overall appearance

Package your report so that it looks and feels good. Design a cover that is bold and that is instantly recognizable. Your organization may have pre-designed covers, in which case you will be constrained in what you can do. If you have a choice, go for a bold title in 36 or 48 point type. Put the author's name prominently on the cover and include, if appropriate, the name of the organization in which you carried out the research.

At this point it might be worth injecting an aside about authorship. When more than one person has been involved in a research project, the attribution of authorship can become a contentious issue. The fairest rule is the one which states that the person who has written the largest part of the report should be given first authorship. This means that their name will appear first on the cover and the title page and whenever the report is cited.

Some unscrupulous researchers try to claim first authorship on other grounds – that they are the senior member of the team, or that they have made the biggest contribution to the intellectual development of the project – even though they have not written the bulk of the report. They should be ashamed of themselves. Authorship means authorship and should be credited accordingly.

If possible, use some bold colour to help make the report look distinctive. Choose a binding that will be robust and will enable readers to lie the report flat. Comb or spiral binders are probably the best. Avoid the heat-sealed binders that glue the pages into a preformed cover – unless they are done very carefully the pages tend to fall out when the report gets a little battered.

Inside the cover have a title page. Many reports go straight to the contents page but people are accustomed to the design conventions of books and they will be expecting a cover and a separate title page. This should repeat all the information on the cover, perhaps adding further details like a subtitle, date of publication and so on.

Next comes the contents page. This should list all the chapters and the main headings. It might sometimes be useful to list all the subheadings as well but this can make it rather cluttered. A full contents page will be really useful. It will help people get an overall feel for the report before they start reading, it will help them navigate their way around and it will serve as a means of retrieving specific items of information.

The page layout

Think about how your pages of text will look. Do everything you can to make it easy for the reader to absorb the messages. This means using quite a lot of white space to give emphasis to the text. Use wide margins – at least one-and-a-half inches or four centimetres – perhaps making the left-hand margin wider so that readers can use it for making notes.

Wide margins like this will mean that you have about the right line length – research has shown that people can easily absorb about 70 or 80 characters in a line and, with 12-point type, this is about the number you will get with four-centimetre margins. Do not justify the right-hand edge of the text. This tends to produce odd spacing between your words and fully justified text is more diffi-cult to read. Leave a blank line between paragraphs and start new chapters on a new page.

Use a consistent style for tables and graphics. If you decide to use two-dimen-sional bar charts stick to these unless absolutely necessary, otherwise people will think that there is something significant in the change of style.

Good research deserves to be presented in a package that is both attractive and effective.

SUMMARY

The nature of the report should be determined by the project itself and by the audience to which the report is addressed. Most reports, no matter what their size or formality, follow a common basic structure. You must say why the work was done, what events led up to it and what other work was relevant. You must state the aim and objectives and describe what you did in order to achieve the objectives. This leads you through to the results, the conclusions you draw from the results and then to the recommendations.

The key to success is thinking the whole report through before you begin writing, building up a detailed outline of the contents. Start with the main chapters, then decide on the main headings within each chapter then the sub-headings. Make sure that everything is covered and dealt with in the most appropriate order. Decide on the length of the completed report and allocate words to each chapter and main heading.

Write clearly and simply, following simple, commonsense principles:

- Be clear about the audience for the report
- Do not assume prior knowledge
- Write as if explaining the points to a panel of readers sitting opposite
- Try to 'sell' the information
- Try to tell a story
- Use words learned early in life
- Avoid initials and acronyms
- Keep sentences short and simple
- Keep the structure simple
- Use no more than three levels of heading
- Use the active rather than the passive voice
- Aim to get it right first time, but be prepared to redraft.

A good report deserves to be presented in a good package. Design an attractive cover. Follow it by a title page and a full list of the report's contents. Design a page layout that is attractive and that will enable the reader to absorb the messages easily and with little effort.

8
Disseminate the results

To get the full value from your research you must be prepared to disseminate the results. You need to communicate information about the research and its results to those people and organizations that can make use of it. The art of good dissemination lies in your ability to select the dissemination channels that best suit the subject of the research and the nature of the audience.

Dissemination does not begin when the report is produced – you can start the process right from the outset of the project, alerting people to the existence of the research and preparing them for the eventual release of the results.

When thinking about dissemination it helps to think of three different audiences. The first have a stake in the research itself. They are actively awaiting the results and will want to see the full report. This group includes the research funders and all the people and organizations that are expected to take some action as a result of the work.

It is not difficult to disseminate to this group. They are receptive and, providing that they know that the report exists, you do not have to put much effort into selling it to them. Sad to say, for most projects, this first group is unfortunately never very large.

The second group consists of the people and organizations that will find something of value and interest in the report but who will not go out of their way to find a copy. You have to sell the report quite hard to this group. You must encourage them to consider the results and, if necessary, to act on the recommendations. Once their interest is aroused, members of this group will want the full report.

The third group may be interested in the subject of the research and might want to know a little about your work and what you found out. They will not really want to bother with the full report but could well be sufficiently interested to read a journal article based on it or to listen to a conference presentation. It is possible that, once they learn a little more about the research, they will follow it up and could well end up looking at the full report. But you will have to work quite hard to get them involved.

So, your dissemination strategy should aim: to make sure that the first group get the full report as quickly as possible; to provide the second with an interesting summary and a means of getting hold of a full report; and to alert the third group to the existence of the research in the hope that some may follow it up later. You can use a number of approaches to get your message across.

Summary findings and press releases

Here the aim is to communicate the main messages contained in the report in order to alert people to its existence and, more generally, to excite people's interest.

Your raw material is the report summary. Sometimes you can take it as it stands, reproduce it as a four- or six-page leaflet and post or e-mail it out to all the people you know to be interested in the research along with an order form for the report itself. You can use the same summary, as a courtesy, to send to people who have contributed to the research by taking part in a focus group or by being interviewed. Your funder and other organizations associated with the work may also be able to distribute copies of the summary on your behalf. Put the summary up on your website.

You can cast the net a little wider by producing a press release to stimulate interest in the media. Just which bit of the media will depend on the nature of the research. It might be local papers and radio stations, the professional press or just occasionally the national press and media.

Begin the press release with a snappy, eye-catching first sentence that will encourage both editors to use the piece and readers to read it. The whole release should run to no more than a single side and should include a quote from you so that it looks as if the paper or the radio station has taken the trouble to get in touch with you. Any background information on the research can be included in notes to editors at the end.

Try to write the release so that it can be shortened from the bottom up. If the editor does not have sufficient space, they will first try to chop off the last paragraph. Decide on a date and time when the report is to be formally published and embargo the press release until that time. This is an informal arrangement whereby the press agree not to use the release before the embargoed time. It may not be critical for your report but it does help to make the release look professional.

Dealing with the media

If you are lucky, or if your research is topical, you may find yourself being approached by the media. This is usually flattering and a bit scary, especially if the approach comes from the national media.

Remember that you are in a position of mutual benefit. The journalist will be doing you a favour but you are also helping them so do not be overawed. Try to keep control of the situation. If you feel you need a little time to think, ask to ring them back – if they press you, say that you need to get clearance from your press office.

Work out precisely what the message is that you want to get over. It is a bit like sorting out the aim of the project right at the beginning. What you want is a single, clear unambiguous sentence that sums it all up and which provides a platform from which you can elaborate on the key points. Try to identify, and articulate, two or three messages that you want to get across. Write them down so that you can have them in front of you when you are talking to the journalist. Try also to think through the difficult questions that you might be asked. Work out suitable responses. When you feel confident, ring the journalist back.

Interviews with journalists can be on or off the record. In circumstances like this, you would be well advised to assume that everything is on the record unless you ask in advance for it not to be – and the journalist agrees. In other words, the journalist will feel able to quote you in anything they write or produce. Listen to the questions that they ask you but to not feel duty-bound to answer them. Rather treat them as opportunities for you to get your two or three points across. Unless the topic is very contentious the journalist will not mind if their question is not answered in precisely the form they posed it.

Then sit back and wait until the article or the interview surfaces. You can then marvel at how it was that they managed to turn something so straightforward into the confused piece that eventually appears.

Conference papers

Conferences are a very good way of communicating with your three audiences. If your work is well known you may receive invitations to speak. If you do not, look ahead to the conferences that are coming up and offer to give a paper. Most conference organizers are delighted to receive an offer out of the blue and will often accept, even if it means squeezing you into a programme that is already full.

Focus the paper on three things: why the research was necessary, what you found and what conclusions you drew. Avoid lengthy discussions of your methods, unless the conference is focused on research methods. Avoid also very full presentations of your results. People will be more interested in the conclusions that you have drawn.

Keep the presentation brief. If the organizer has allowed you 30 minutes, plan a presentation that will last no more than 20 – they always take rather longer on the day than you expect and no-one was ever criticized for giving a presentation that was too short. Try to make it sound interesting. When speaking put as much emphasis as you can into your voice. Never read a paper. You may have to produce a written paper in advance but discard it when it comes to making the presentation.

Make some notes outlining what it is that you are going to say. Work out an interesting opening sentence and a resounding concluding one and write those out to provide yourself with a safe entrance and exit. Then, for the bits in-between, produce notes from which you can speak. It will make the presentation live much more and the adrenalin produced by the sheer terror of standing up before 200 people with only a few notes to protect you will carry you through.

Support your presentation with a few simple visual aids. Overhead projector transparencies are safe. Computer-generated presentations using software like Powerpoint are a little more risky but they have now become the norm. Keep each slide simple, usually with a heading and three or four bullet points. Ration yourself to 20 words per slide – never use more words than you would expect to find on the front of a tee-shirt. If you are using a computer, try not to make it too gimmicky – it will only detract from the message you are trying to communicate. Practise the presentation and the use of the visual aids until you are confident. Remember the adage about musicians – good amateurs practise until they get it right, professionals practise until they never get it wrong. And then go for it – knock 'em dead in the aisles.

Journal articles

Here you need to draw a distinction between professional periodicals and more scholarly, academic journals. The latter will send your article out for refereeing and it may not appear for months. Professional periodicals, on the other hand, have much shorter timescales and will aim to turn things around more quickly.

Professional periodicals

To appear in a professional periodical you first have to convince the editor that you have something to say that will interest the readers. You could draft an article and send it in asking for it to be published. It would be better, though, to telephone the editor and to talk through what your research was about. The editor will be able to give you an indication of whether or not the idea is suitable. They will also be in a position to advise you on the line to take, or the areas to avoid. They will know what their readers are interested in and they will be able to steer you towards something that will produce an impact. Critically, they will be able to tell you how many words they require and when they will need them.

When writing the article, make it as interesting as possible. Use case studies and individual examples. Try to personalize it, showing what impact your research, or the issue you have been exploring, has on an individual or a family. Try to find some illustrations or graphics that can liven up the text.

Academic journals

For academic journals bury all your journalistic instincts as deep as you can. The primary aim of academic journals is to communicate the products of scientific (in the broadest sense) endeavour to the scholarly community. To do this, a particular style of writing and presentation has evolved and you will need to conform to it.

The first thing to do is to identify the most appropriate journal. Clearly you want one that covers the same subject area as your research. You will also want one that is prestigious, perhaps with an international audience. The only problem with these is that they usually receive more papers than they can publish. It might be better to opt for a less well known journal, perhaps one with a more limited geographical circulation.

The key characteristic of academic journals is the use of peer review to ensure quality. All papers received are sent out to at least two referees who comment on the quality of the work and its suitability for publication. They will almost certainly be academics approaching the paper from an academic standpoint. To succeed you must conform. You must write in an academic style. For those unaccustomed to it, this can be very stilted and hard to comprehend. You will have to set aside all you have learned about clear writing and plain English and instead, conform to the style of other authors in the journal.

You must also comply with the publication requirements of the journal. These are usually set out in detail inside the front or back cover of the journal. They will guide you on matters of length, bibliographical citation and so on.

For the structure of the paper, think of it as a condensed version of your final report – introduction, methods, results, conclusions and recommendations. Produce something of the correct length and submit it to the editor. Within a month or two you should receive the referees' comments back. Assuming they are broadly positive, you will be asked to revise the paper and to resubmit. You may then have to wait anything up to two years for your article to appear.

SUMMARY

The art of good dissemination lies in your ability to select the dissemination channels that best suit the subject of the research and the nature of the audience.

It is often useful to adapt the report summary and issue it as a free-standing summary of the research, mailing it out to the people and organizations you think will be interested. You can also issue a press release to draw attention to the research and its report. When dealing with the media, remember that the benefit is mutual. Try to retain the initiative and be clear about the messages that you want to convey.

Persuade conference organizers to let you present a paper based on your research. Keep things simple and focus on the need for the research and on the findings and conclusions. Do not read a paper; instead, train yourself to speak from notes. Use visual aids but keep them simple.

Produce articles for professional periodicals and academic journals. But understand that a different approach is required for each.

SUMMARY

... ...
... ...
... ...
... ...
... ...
... ...
... ...

... ...
... ...
... ...
... ...

... ...
... ...

Part 2
Methods

9
Introducing research methods

Methods are the tools of the researcher's trade. You need to know how to use them but, just as important, is knowing when they should be used. The perfect researcher will be familiar with the widest possible range of methods and will deploy them selectively to meet the requirements of different circumstances.

For the rest of us, our aspirations are more modest. Most of us can only hope to be familiar with a limited range of methods, understanding their strengths and weaknesses and being aware of when to use one in preference to another. With luck, we will also know that there are lots of other different ways of approaching the collection and analysis of data and we will be in a position to identify when we need to extend our personal range of skills by learning to use a new method.

This part of the book aims to give you an overview of the range of social research methods that are available to you. It will indicate the strengths and weaknesses of each method and will suggest when and under which circumstances, they should be used. It will also give you some hints and tips that will help you get going. What it will not do is provide a detailed treatise on social research methods in all their sophisticated glory. There are plenty of other books that do this. Some of them have even been written by people who have actually used the methods. A selection of them is listed in the guide to further reading in Chapter 16.

At this point it is worth saying a word about triangulation. Many researchers use only one method at a time to collect data – the research project will consist of a questionnaire survey, or a series of focus groups. There is, however, much to be gained by using more than one method to explore an issue from different perspectives. A relatively large scale questionnaire survey will, for example, provide a broad picture. This picture can be enriched by a series of focus groups to explore aspects of the topic in more depth. The whole thing can be put into a wider context by a thorough review of the literature and consideration of the results of previous research on the topic. The jargon term for looking at things in this way is triangulation.

Most social research involves collecting data about the subject in which you are interested. The data then needs to be analysed and interpreted for you to be able to arrive at your conclusions.

At this point it is worth clarifying some of the terms used. Data are bits of information that, on their own, have no value or meaning. When data are processed and analysed they can be converted into information that has value and meaning. The research process is, therefore, concerned with collecting data and processing it into information. People can use the information thus created to add to their knowledge, perhaps even developing wisdom.

Thus '23 per cent' is *data*; '23 per cent of the population aged under 60 use the public library at least once a month' is *information*; 'but half of them only go in to use the toilets' is *knowledge*; while 'so all public libraries should contain toilets if they want to attract extra visitors' is *wisdom*.

Collecting data

Most social researchers recognize a distinction between the use of quantitative and qualitative methods for collecting data. Quantitative methods collect information about things that you can count – such as the proportion of people in the population who would vote for one political party compared with another, or the number of people in a community who feel strongly about a particular form of public service.

Qualitative research is concerned with information about things that are less easily understood by counting them – such as the strategies that people who live on low incomes adopt to make their incomes stretch as far as possible, or the attitudes that managers have towards the motivation of their staff.

While this is a useful distinction, the dividing line between the two types of methods is not clear-cut. Quantitative research techniques have become very sophisticated and it is possible to take a quantitative approach to many issues that are qualitative in nature. You can, for example, use a quantitative approach towards the measurement of people's attitudes and strengths of belief. We will, however, follow convention and look at quantitative measures separately from those that are qualitative.

These methods are concerned with the collection of new data. There is also much that can be done with the wealth of data and information that already exists. Most good research projects begin with a review of this existing data and information – a process commonly known as desk research. So we will begin with a section devoted to desk research and the collection of existing data.

Analysis - converting data into information

Once you have collected the data you have to do something with it and there are various ways you can do this. First you have to process the data, checking its accuracy and getting it into a form which will enable you to analyse it. Increasingly this means processing it by computer.

Then, once the data are organized, you can begin to make sense of it all, interpreting the findings and converting the data into information. This is the really difficult bit.

SUMMARY

Methods are the tools of the researcher's trade. You need to know how to use them but just as important is knowing when they should be used. Readers looking for a detailed treatment of methods should consult one or more of the books listed in Chapter 16. Here they will find a simple overview.

Social research methods can be grouped in two broad categories: those that are concerned with collecting data and those that are used to convert data into information. In both cases the categories can be further subdivided into quantitative, qualitative and desk research methods. Most good research projects begin with desk research to collect and analyse the data and information that already exists.

10
Desk research

Not all research is about collecting new data – or primary data as it is known in the trade. A great deal can be achieved by working with data that have already been collected and processed by others. Indeed, most good research begins with a review of what has gone before. This type of research is often referred to as desk research.

Some projects are solely concerned with desk research, relying entirely on the re-analysis of other people's research or on secondary analysis of data that have been collected by others. Even the research that is based on the collection of primary data usually has an element of desk research built in. Few researchers, for example, feel able to manage without some form of literature review or contextual work to position their research.

Desk research covers a range of activities. Literature reviews are the most common. Increasingly the term 'literature' needs to be expanded to include material found on the internet. Closely allied to these reviews, and growing in importance, are research reviews which focus on the analysis of actual research findings from a number of different studies. There is also secondary analysis of data where the focus is firmly on the reworking of existing data sets to develop new insights into issues.

This chapter concentrates on the collection of the material used in desk research. The analytical techniques will be dealt with in Chapter 11.

Literature and internet searching

This is a very important part of nearly all research projects, yet it is something that is often dealt with superficially.

No research project exists in isolation. Each piece of work relates in some way to the environment within which the research takes place, to the theories and concepts that have been developed to explain the environmental conditions and to other research on the topic. If your work is to have coherence and relevance you should take full account of what has gone before and what is going on around you. You therefore need to make sure you are fully aware of all the relevant literature on the subject.

You will have carried out a limited review in order to produce your proposal. You will probably be aware of the main issues and policies, you may be able to cite the principal theories that others have developed and you may even be in touch with other researchers working in the field. But once you get the go-ahead for the research you need to make sure that the knowledge you bring to the project is complete and up to date. To do this you will need to search the literature.

When planning your literature search it is often helpful to think about what types of material you are looking for. Your will probably be interested in three things: the policy context, the theories and the research. They may be inter-related, but fundamentally they are different and you may have to look for them in different places.

You should then think carefully about the subject boundaries of your search. If we return to the example of research into training and organizational change, you might be looking for material on training, organizational change, attitudes to change and motivation. You might be interested in big organizations, small organizations, multinationals or organizations in the public and voluntary sectors. You might be interested in what has happened in the last few years or you might want to take a much longer perspective.

Here it is useful to introduce the concepts of recall and relevance. In any collection of material there will be a finite number of items that will be of interest to you. To retrieve these you can cast your net wide in order to be sure that you *recall* all the materials that might be of use. But if you do this you will find that you retrieve quite a lot of less useful material which you then have to discard. An alternative approach is to narrow the search down so that you increase the chances that the material will be *relevant*, but, if you do this, you increase the risk that you will miss something. The trick is to balance the breadth of recall with the depth of relevance.

Most people do this by starting out with fairly broad search terms. You can then look at the results and identify the materials that look to be most useful. You can then refine the search accordingly so that you increase the relevance of the search.

The mechanics

The mechanics of searching for published literature have improved beyond measure in the last ten years or so. You no longer face the job of wading through annual volumes of printed indexes and abstracts, looking for the same search terms over and over again. Now you can do it all at the touch of a button – well, almost. Computerized databases have transformed literature searching, but they have not necessarily made it easier. If you are doing this sort of thing for the first time, then you would be well advised to seek the help of a fully trained librarian or information specialist.

The first task is to identify the most suitable databases to search. You might look in the catalogue of a large or specialist library. This will be good for identifying books and research reports, but will not be much use for identifying journal articles. For these you will need to search specialist databases providing indexes and, more usefully, abstracts of journal articles. These databases are usually accessible online or on CD-ROM. In either case, you will need to get at them through a subscribing library. You can do a limited amount over the internet but the really useful material is likely to be found through subscriber-only databases.

If you have to do the searching yourself, plan the search carefully. List the keywords that you will be searching for. Think about the need to truncate them – most databases enable you to use a symbol to truncate a word so that you increase the rate of recall. For example, instead of just searching for 'motivation' you search for 'motivat*' which will retrieve the words 'motivate', 'motivates', 'motivation', motivational', 'motivations' and so on.

Think about synonyms. For 'organizations' you might also need to search for 'institutions', 'corporations', 'companies' and 'corporate bodies'. You will also need to allow for different spellings – 'organizations' can be spelled with an 's' or a 'z'.

Then you need to grapple with Boolean logic. This enables you to structure your search more precisely. Unfortunately the application of Boolean principles varies slightly from database to database and you will need to check that you are doing things properly. Essentially, though, Boolean logic enables you to create a search that will, for example, retrieve articles in which the words 'organizations', 'training', 'motivation' and 'change' all appear in the same sentence, or all appear somewhere in the article.

But here we are beginning to get a little technical and novices should seek help from the specialists. Once you get the hang of it, you can do wonderful things – but you can also find yourself tied up in knots, retrieving thousands of items or none at all.

Developing the search

As you search, look at the results and use them to refine things. Try to see what searches have produced the most – and the least – interesting material and re-structure your searches accordingly. Look at the results on the screen and play around with the searches until you are reasonably sure you have got the balance between recall and relevance about right; then start printing them out. You should aim for a manageable number of items – how many will depend on the nature and size of the research project. Just remember that you will need to read the documents at some stage.

Once you have identified the documents, you then need your librarian to get hold of them for you. As the material arrives, look at it to see where it leads you. Check the citations and the bibliographies. Do they point to material that you have not identified? If so, get hold of those documents too. Sooner or later you should find that you keep coming back to the same materials – you will have identified the core and should be able to specify which among these are the key documents.

If you are working on a big project you may compile a large list of material, in which case you may need to create a database of your own, assigning key-words to the documents to enable you to retrieve them easily.

Internet searching

The internet is a wonderful thing. For those of us who grew up with printed indexes, abstracts and bibliographies, the internet is astonishingly liberating. It enables researchers gain access to material that previously it would have been difficult to trace and even harder to obtain. I have just completed, for example, a review of information policies in the Asian region. I was able to identify and download hundreds of documents, pieces of legislation, statistical analyses, reviews and commentaries from nearly 30 countries stretching from Iran to Japan. And I was able to do it all without moving from my desk.

The only problem is that people born after the early 1980s tend to think that if they cannot find something on the internet, then it does not exist!

A good way to structure an internet search is to begin by identifying relevant portals and gateways. These are websites that provide access to relevant internet-based resources. A good example is one that I used for my review of information policies: the Unesco Observatory on the Information Society (http://portal.unesco.org/ci/en/ev.php-URL_ID=7277&URL_DO=DO_TOPIC &URL_SECTION=201.html). This lists, region-by-region and then country-by-country, a wide range of material contained in different websites.

Portals like this enable you to go quickly to relevant websites. Once there, you can begin to dig around to find the information that you need. Some portals go a little further and evaluate the websites and their contents.

Portals alone, however, will not be sufficient – they are only as good as the information that is posted on them. You should supplement your search using search engines like Google and Yahoo. To get the best out of these tools it is well worth learning to use their advanced search features, as they will enable you to structure your searches, reducing the level of recall while boosting the relevance of the results. The strategies for searching are much the same as for searching more conventional bibliographic databases, as discussed above.

One thing to remember is that the item that you are looking for may not appear on the first two or three pages of thre search results, particularly if you are looking for something obscure. Persevere and work your way systematically through the results, trying, as you go, to identify ways in which you can refine your search.

Statistical data

Much desk research involves the secondary analysis of statistical data. The sources of the data vary considerably.

Some of the most frequently used are the data sets produced by government statisticians from the regular surveys that they carry out on almost everything from the state of the national economy to the incidence of crime. In Britain, the Office for National Statistics is responsible for collecting and managing these data sets and they publish details of what is available on their website at: **www.statistics.gov.uk**. These government statistics are a goldmine and a great deal can be done to apply them in a variety of different circumstances.

Then there are the data sets that have been created by other research projects. In Britain the Economic and Social Research Council maintains the UK Data Archive at Essex University (**www.data-archive.ac.uk/**) and all research projects funded by the Research Council and by a number of other funders are required to lodge their datasets in the archive where they can be used by others.

Clearly, you need to know what you are looking for when thinking about using this kind of statistical data. You need to check the data carefully to make sure it covers the topics that you are interested in, but, more importantly, that it is structured in ways that will be of use to you.

Once you have identified the dataset that you are interested in, you need to negotiate access. In Britain, members of the academic community can gain access at preferential rates through the Joint Academic Network. Other people have more restricted access and may need to negotiate on a case-by-case basis.

SUMMARY

A great deal can be achieved through desk research, working with data that has already been collected and processed by others.

Desk research covers a range of activities. Literature and internet reviews are the most common. Closely allied to these, and growing in importance, are research reviews which focus on the analysis of actual research findings from a number of different studies. There is also secondary analysis of data where the focus is firmly on the reworking of existing data sets to develop new insights into issues.

Just about all projects require a review of published literature and internet resources to position the work in its proper context. When searching for the material to review you need to find the best balance between recall and relevance. The mechanics of searching have improved greatly with the development of computer-based bibliographical databases and the internet. But searching can be a skilled task and novices are strongly recommended to seek the help of a trained information specialist.

Secondary analysis of existing datasets is a powerful research technique and a great deal of research data is available for this kind of analysis. The secret lies in identifying the most appropriate datasets.

11
Analysing desk research

Desk research can call for quantitative or qualitative approaches to analysis. Clearly, if you are embarking on the secondary analysis of data, then you will need to follow the same kind of approach that you would if you had collected the data yourself.

If, on the other hand, you are analysing the results of a literature or internet search or you are conducting a review of research, you will need to adopt approaches that draw heavily on qualitative research.

Common principles

There are, however, some principles that are common to the analysis of all desk research.

Authority and reliability

You need to begin by questioning the authority and reliability of the material you are working with. If you have collected the data yourself you will have a reasonable idea of the amount of trust you can place in it. If someone else has compiled the data then you need to look fairly carefully at how they did it.

You need to look at sample sizes and the basis for drawing the samples. You should, if you can, look at the data collection tools used – the questionnaires, interview schedules and so on. You should give some thought to the people who conducted the research – how much experience do they have, are they known to you, would you trust them? Clearly, data produced from one of the regular government social surveys will have a different standing from that produced as part of an independent study carried out by an unknown research team.

If you are dealing with published material, what authority does the publisher bring to the party? What steps will they have taken to ensure that the research is worth publishing? Similar questions could be applied to the research sponsor.

Be clear about what you are looking for

A structured approach to the material you have to work with is much more likely to bear fruit. Work out in advance what it is that you are interested in. At first you may only have a broad idea derived from your project aim and objectives. As you work through the material, develop a more refined set of issues and questions that you want to explore. At any stage in the process you should be able to state quite clearly what it is that you are looking for in your material.

Be organized and systematic

Try hard to adopt an organized approach to the material. Keep things well documented. If you are reviewing material collected through a literature or internet search, keep all the printouts, books and copies of journal articles easily accessible. You should have a record of what material you have to hand, what material you have decided not to look at and what is on its way from different libraries. Try to organize the material systematically into different categories so that you can structure your analysis better. Keep a note of the website addresses you have used.

Document things as you go

Keep full notes of what you find when you go through the material. You will always need to refer back to the source documents, but your notes should provide you with most of what you need to know. If you are looking at different published sources, keep notes on each book, article or report, but think also of the issues that you are exploring. Note down any quotes that encapsulate ideas or concepts so that you can use them when you come to write up the report.

When you have been through all the materials, work from your notes and transpose them so that they are structured around the issues you are exploring.

Comparison is critical

As with other forms of data analysis, comparison is the key. You are looking for similarities and differences between the materials you are working with. On what issues do they agree? Where are there differences?

Analysis and synthesis

You first have to analyse the material, breaking it down into its component parts – segmenting it. But, having done this, your task is then to synthesize the results, bringing things together and noting where there are significant differences. Your eventual aim should be to produce something that increases our understanding of the issues – a synthesis where the whole is greater than the sum of the parts.

SUMMARY

The analytical techniques used in desk research are similar to those used for the analysis of quantitative and qualitative data. They should be based on six simple principles:

* Check the authority and reliability
* Be clear about what you are looking for
* Be organized and systematic
* Document things as you go
* Comparison is critical
* Use both analysis and synthesis.

12
Collecting quantitative data

For many people, collecting quantitative data is the core of social research. Types of quantitative techniques are the things that first come to mind when people think of social research – techniques such as self-completion questionnaires and interview surveys. They are all founded on the principle that you can generate information about the characteristics of a group by collecting data from a subset of that group.

This principle was developed first by researchers in the natural sciences. They carried out experiments and measured the results. The experiments were then repeated many times until the researchers could be sure that the results they obtained were not the product of random chance but were characteristic of the subjects or objects they were studying. This approach has been subsequently adapted by social scientists and it underpins all quantitative methods.

Sampling

Let's face it, sampling is difficult. The basic principle is straightforward: you take a sample from a large group, look in detail at that sample and then infer the characteristics of the whole group from those of the sample. Of course, it is not quite that simple. You can never be sure that the sample has the same characteristics as the group – they probably do, but you cannot be certain. So you have to allow for that degree of probability.

Sample size

You need a sample that is big enough to represent all the characteristics of the larger group. In part, this depends on the relative size of the group and the sample you select. Let us suppose that you are trying to measure the proportion of people in the population who have brown hair and blue eyes. You walk down the street and the tenth person you meet has brown hair and blue eyes. Can you infer from this that ten per cent of the population have brown hair and blue eyes? Probably not.

So you walk on and look at 100 people. Of these, eight have brown hair and blue eyes. So, is the proportion eight per cent? Well possibly, but to be a little more certain you carry on walking until you have passed 1000 people. By now you have counted 78 people with brown hair and blue eyes. You can fairly confidently say that about eight per cent of the population have the brown hair–blue eye combination. You might improve your confidence by looking at the next 5000 people you meet, but it is unlikely to make much difference.

So, the size of the sample is important. If, for example, 50 per cent of the population you are interested in have brown hair and you take a sample of 100 people you can be 95 per cent certain that you will find that between 40 and 60 per cent of your sample have brown hair. Increase the sample to 1000 people and you will find between 47 and 53 per cent have brown hair. Increase it again to 10,000 and the range reduces further to between 49 and 51 per cent. The bigger the sample, the more likely the results are to be representative of the whole population.

Random samples

The way you choose the sample can also be important. If you are trying to measure the colour of people's hair and eyes, it probably does not matter how you select your sample – walking down the street is as good as any approach. But supposing you wanted to measure the proportion of the population who spend more than 60 minutes each month using a mobile telephone. Selecting people you meet in the street is a little bit unreliable. You will come across very few people who spend most of their lives indoors but very many people who are out and about for much of the day. Use of mobile telephones is likely to be affected by whether you live your life indoors or out, and so your sample is unlikely to represent the characteristics of the population as a whole and this could distort your results.

To overcome the problem you must try to pick a sample that is representative and to do this you have to select the group randomly from the whole population you want to survey. Picking people in the street is not random. For the sample to be random everyone in the sample must have an equal chance, or probability, of being selected.

Sampling frames

To select randomly, you need to begin with a list of the whole group to be sampled, known in the trade as a sampling frame; and in this context the group to be sampled is known as the population. This might be the list of employees within a firm or a list of students at a university. Once you have the list you can select your sample.

It is really important to begin by making sure that your sampling frame is accurate: is the list of employees up-to-date? Does the list of students contain the names of all those who enrolled or just those who are still on the course? If you are dealing with surveys of organizations, you may need to compile your own sampling frame, using address lists and directories. Again, you need to ask whether the list is comprehensive, accurate and up-to-date. Compiling an accurate sampling frame like this can be both time-consuming and frustrating but it is essential if your sampling is to be accurate and your results statistically significant.

This is just as valid if you are going to survey the whole population, without drawing a sample. Essentially, you need to know that you have included everyone, or every organization in the population, because, unless you have, you cannot be sure that your results will be statistically significant. I recently worked on a survey of libraries, museums and archives in a region of England. We had to compile our own sampling frame by updating an existing address list using information from a wide range of different sources. For various reasons we did not do a very good job and we ended up sending questionnaires to lots of organizations that did not have libraries, museums or archives. We also probably missed some that did. Sorting out the resultant problems at the analysis stage took an inordinate amount of time and effort.

It is more difficult with the general population. In most countries there is no single, fully accurate list of people. In Britain, the best we can do is to use the electoral register but this is only updated annually and does not take account of homeless people. The Post Office maintains an address file which lists all the houses and flats where people live. This is fine if you are surveying households but it is not much good if you are surveying individuals as people who live alone will have twice the chance of being selected as people who live in two-person households. However, for surveys of the general population it is usually necessary to use one of these lists and to accept the imperfections that result.

Once you have your sampling frame you can select your sample. If the list is numbered you could use a table of random numbers to select your sample. Or you could select every fifth, tenth or twentieth person, according to the size of the sample you need. These approaches will give you what is known as a pure random sample or a random probability sample. The problem with them is that they are difficult to operate and can give you a sample that is spread all over the country and is thus expensive to survey.

Stratified or cluster samples

To overcome this, you can stratify the sample. With this technique you divide the sampling frame into mutually exclusive groups. If you were sampling the whole population of a country, for example, you could divide the population into geographical areas like local authority areas or census enumeration districts. These could then be stratified according to key variables, such as the proportion of people who are unemployed. You would list all the areas with an unemployment rate of below three per cent, those with between three and five per cent, and so on. You could then select a random sample of these areas; this would give you a stratified sampling frame from which you could select your random sample of survey respondents. Using this approach, you ensure that the people you want to survey are clustered together in a number of areas rather than spread over the whole country, making it much easier to get at them. This form of sampling is sometimes referred to as cluster sampling.

Quota samples

Quota samples are rather different from random probability samples. In a quota sample people do not have an equal probability of being selected. Instead, you decide in advance which types of people you want to survey and how many of each type, and you then set about finding them.

On the surface, quota samples are similar to stratified samples: an interviewer is given certain quotas to be filled – they must, for example, interview 25 women aged over 40 or 15 people who have bought a book in the last week. But the difference is that it is left to the interviewer's discretion which women or book buyers they select.

If the whole population is being surveyed, the quotas may be selected to reflect the population. If, for example, 28 per cent of the whole population are working women between the ages of 20 and 60 and the sample size is 1000, then the interviewers will be told to find 280 working women between the ages of 20 and 60.

The people with clipboards that you keep bumping into in the street are interviewers working on quota samples – the fact that they do not interview you does not mean that you look particularly dangerous or shifty, it is simply that you are not the kind of person who fits the quota they have been given that day.

Quota samples will give you data that is less statistically valid than random samples. Their advantage is that they are cheaper to administer.

Response rate bias

If you rely on people to complete questionnaires and return them to you, your sample can be open to response rate bias. It is just possible that the characteristics of the people who return the questionnaires are different from those who do not and so your sample ceases to be representative of the whole population. Clearly, the higher the response rate, the less chance there is that this will happen, but it can be a problem.

As a basic rule of thumb, you should aim for a response rate of 60 per cent or above. Surveys with response rates of between 50 and 60 per cent should be treated with caution. Below 50 per cent response and you should not really attempt any quantitative analysis as all of your results will be subject to wide margins of statistical error.

Weighting data

You will hear statisticians talking about weighting data. By this they simply mean giving greater prominence to the data from certain groups within the sample in order to give greater statistical representativeness.

Let us say that you want to survey people to find out who would use a telephone-based information service. The service is planned to cover an area in which only 20 per cent of the population live in rural communities. If you sampled 500 people and you chose a random sample you would probably only pick up 100 respondents from rural areas and that would not give you enough to analyse as a separate group.

To overcome this, you over-sample rural areas: that is, you collect information from, probably, 200 people in rural areas. That will give you an overall sample of 300 from urban areas and 200 from rural. Both subsets of data are big enough to warrant statistical analysis. But if you put them together, you will have a sample that is not representative of the whole population – it will be biased to the rural areas. So you weight the data, multiplying the results from urban areas by two in order to bring the balance in the sample back into line with the whole population.

You can also weight data to try to overcome imbalances in response rates. Supposing in the example above, equal numbers of people lived in rural and urban areas but when you looked at the returned questionnaires you found that you had a lot more from urban areas than you did from rural. You could weight the data to redress the imbalance but, in so doing, you could well be masking underlying differences. So this type of weighting is to be treated with caution.

As we said at the beginning, sampling is not easy. It is well worth identifying a sympathetic statistician and asking them for expert advice when you are in doubt. Getting your samples right is the first step towards collecting reliable quantitative data.

Self-completion questionnaire surveys

Self-completion questionnaires are very popular with researchers. They are relatively easy to administer. They are flexible in that they can be used to collect a wide range of data in a variety of different circumstances. And they are relatively cheap.

They can be delivered to the respondents in a variety of different ways. The most common is to post the questionnaires to organizations or to people's home addresses, asking them to complete the questionnaire and return it in an enclosed pre-addressed envelope. In other cases people are handed the questionnaire when they come into contact with a service or a product – you will have come across the survey forms that newspapers and magazines use to collect data about their readers, or surveys that come with products that you buy. Often users of public services will be handed a questionnaire as they leave the building asking for their views. They are probably the most commonly used social research method.

Self-completion questionnaires are good for collecting data on non-contentious and relatively straightforward topics. They are not good for asking about sensitive issues like income or for exploring complex issues or concepts that are hard to define. Few people, for example, have successfully explored information needs using self-completion questionnaires, simply because the concept of 'information' means so many different things to different people.

These questionnaires are also unlikely to produce a great depth of information. People tend to fill them in quickly, giving an immediate rather than a considered response. So use them for building up a broad picture rather than exploring issues in depth.

They are, however, popular among respondents. People can look through them in advance before deciding whether or not to complete them. They can be completed at a convenient time, not just when an interviewer happens to be standing on a doorstep. They also ensure that all respondents have the questions presented to them in a standard way without interviewers introducing any bias.

The biggest problem with them is the response rate that you obtain. For some postal questionnaires this can be very low. For surveys handed out with products and distributed to people using services, the response rates tend to be even lower. This calls into question the statistical validity of data produced and, when response rates drop below 50 per cent, the results should be used only to provide a broad indication of what is happening.

Length

One of the first things you should think about when designing a self-completion questionnaire is its length. This will have a big impact on people's response – the longer the questionnaire, the less likely people are to complete it.

Anything longer than four sides of paper is likely to be too long – people simply cannot be bothered. But what is actually more important than the number of sides of paper is the amount of time it takes to complete the form. Good design can make even a long form easy to fill in. The trick is to tell people right at the beginning how long they will have to spend.

So, ration yourself to a small number of key questions and focus on them.

Closed questions

The easiest questions to handle, for the researcher and the respondent, are closed questions. The respondent is asked a question and required to answer by choosing between a limited number of answers – such questionnaires are often called multiple-choice questionnaires. They are easy to complete and easy to analyse. They provide a range of answers and so reduce the chance of the respondent overlooking something; they also reduce the chance that the respondent will give an ambiguous answer.

Closed questions, however, can only really be used to obtain fairly straightforward, uncomplicated information.

When designing closed questions, make sure that you have provided for all the likely answers and that your choices are mutually exclusive – there should be no ambiguity. Where appropriate, give the respondent space to write in their own answer if it does not fall into one of the categories that you have listed.

The usual format is to ask the question and then to provide the possible answers, asking the respondent to tick the appropriate box. A typical closed question would look like this:

How did you travel to work today?

On foot	❏
By car	❏
By bus	❏
By train	❏
Other, please specify	❏

....

This asks a simple question, presents a number of choices and should be easy to complete. People, however, normally expect to tick a single box – yet some of your respondents may have ridden to the station, travelled by train into the city and then taken a bus. You must allow them to tick more than one response. Do this by adding a note telling them.

An alternative approach would be to present the question and answers in a different way:

Did you make all or part of your journey to work today:

	Yes	No
On foot?	❏	❏
By car?	❏	❏
By bus?	❏	❏
By train?	❏	❏
Other, please specify	❏	

....

This would make life easier for the respondent, but it will make it a little more difficult for you to process the answers.

In some cases a simple 'yes' or 'no' answer is not sufficient. You may be trying to explore shades of opinion or degrees of satisfaction. To do this you can use a rating scale:

How do you feel about these aspects of the hotel?

	Very satisfied	Satisfied	Dissatisfied	Very dissatisfied
Staff	❏	❏	❏	❏
Rooms	❏	❏	❏	❏
Meals	❏	❏	❏	❏

Do not have too many points on your rating scale – four or six is normal – and do not have an odd number – people's natural conformity will encourage them to revert to the middle box when in doubt. Some people also have a tendency to err consistently to one side or another, usually expressing greater satisfaction than they feel. This is known in the trade as a response set and you can counter it, to an extent, by ensuring that 'satisfied' or 'good' does not always appear on the left hand side of the range or that some questions are expressed in a negative way. This will break up the pattern of answers, although it will not overcome people's tendency to conform and to provide the answers they think the researcher wants.

Open questions

To overcome these difficulties, you can use open questions. Here you place the onus on the respondent to formulate answers using their own words. This has obvious limitations. It is only effective when used by people who are happy expressing themselves in writing and doing so succinctly.

Open questions also give you a headache when it comes to processing the completed returns. Somehow you have to impose some kind of order on the results. You do this by compiling a coding frame. You look at the first 20 or 30 responses and list the answers given. Take out duplicates and things that mean the same even though people have expressed them differently and you will be left with the range of answers given by those first 20. Give each of these a number or a code, and then work through all the other responses coding the answers according to the coding frame you have worked out. Instead of imposing the choices on respondents in advance, you are reflecting the answers they have given spontaneously.

The same approach is used to manage the responses to the 'Other, please specify . . .' questions that appear so frequently in closed questionnaires.

Design, layout and phrasing

The golden rule is to keep things short and simple. Prepare your initial draft and expect to reduce it in length by at least 50 per cent.

Once the number, range and scope of the questions have been decided, the next step is to phrase them in a form that is most likely to reflect the true nature of the question, to be understood by the respondent and to produce answers that can be handled by the researcher. This means that you have to keep the wording as simple as possible, avoiding any possibility of ambiguity. Getting the wording right can be a time-consuming business in which you have to pay great attention to detail. But it is well worth it. A well designed questionnaire will help to achieve a good response rate and will do much to create a good impression. Follow some basic principles.

Get the beginning right. You will need a covering letter and we will come to that later, but for those who may discard the letter, make sure that the first thing people see on the questionnaire is a paragraph or statement that will catch their interest and motivate them to fill in the form. It should indicate the problem that the survey has been designed to address and, if possible, it should show

how they will benefit themselves and others by providing the information. You should also tell them how long it is likely to take them to complete the questionnaire.

Make it personal but un-patronizing. Write as if you were talking to the respondent and avoid jargon and the use of initials. Aim for a warm and friendly tone.

Use simple words. Choose those words that you learned early in life. The word 'form', for example, is more easily understood than 'questionnaire'. When faced with two possible words, it usually pays to choose the shortest.

Keep the sentences short. You will be trying to keep the questions short, but apply the same discipline to the notes and explanations on the form. Resist the temptation to shorten sentences by taking out the words like 'a', 'the' and 'that' which hold the sentence together and help it make sense.

Keep the sentence construction simple. Try to follow the usual English word order of subject, verb and object. Avoid having more than two clauses in a sentence. Use the active voice – it sounds better than saying 'the active voice of the verb should be used'. Use basic punctuation. In questionnaires it should seldom be necessary to use anything other than commas and full stops.

Use a large enough type size. Ten point is about the minimum – 12 point is better. If you are surveying older people, consider increasing the type size to 14 point. Leave people enough space to write things in.

Avoid using block capitals. They may make something stand out but, in fact, words printed in capitals are more difficult to read than words in lower case. People read by recognizing the shape of words and blocked type reduces the differences in shapes between words. If you need to emphasize anything, use italics or bold type.

Make it look attractive. Be a little fussy and aim for perfection. Remember once the questionnaire is issued it will be too late to make alterations, so you have got to get it right. It will look better, for example, if all the tick boxes are aligned and if there is plenty of space between questions.

Avoid introducing bias through the phrasing of your questions. Avoid writing things like:

Should teachers be held responsible for maintaining cultural and educational standards?

Would you like the opening hours to be increased?

Many people think that traffic speeds should be reduced – do you agree?

Avoid the use of negatives – people are much happier when thinking about positives. Try this, for example:

Do you think that opening hours should not be reduced?

A light touch is desirable but look out for unintentional gaffes, like the government survey that asked for details of employees 'broken down by age and sex'.

When planning the sequence of questions try to ensure that each flows from the one before and onto the one that follows. If there is a definite break, signal this with a small phrase like 'Now, turning to . . .' Work from the general to the specific.

If you plan to process the data by computer, remember to number each answer or response so that when the returns come in the data can be inputted easily.

Skips and filters

Try to ensure that all respondents can answer all the questions. If this is not possible, use skips and filters to help people navigate around the questionnaire. You usually do this by asking a 'yes/no' question to begin with and then directing people accordingly:

Do you have children between the ages of 5 and 16?   Yes/No
If Yes, proceed to question 2
If No, skip questions 2–6 and proceed directly to question 7

To help people find question 7 you can put an arrow down the margin.

Use notes to define concepts and to clarify possible ambiguities. Try to place the note as close to the question as possible, while avoiding a cluttered look to the questionnaire. If you have phrased your questions carefully you should not need many notes.

Think about how you are going to handle the completed questionnaires once they have been returned. If the results are going to be punched for computer analysis you should take advice from the agency that will be doing the punching. You will probably need to give each response a number, for example.

Try to make the questionnaire look as if it has been professionally printed. For some reason a questionnaire printed on both sides of an A3 sheet and then folded to make an A4 booklet looks smaller than the same number of sheets stapled together. It is also easier to handle and there is less chance of sheets becoming detached.

If appropriate, give the name of someone to whom the respondent can refer if they have any queries with the questionnaire or need to follow anything up.

Anonymity

It is highly desirable to promise anonymity. People are more likely to respond if they think the information will be treated in confidence and that their names will not be recorded. This can be tricky, however. If replies are anonymous, you do not know who to send reminder letters to. One way around this is to number the questionnaires, record who receives which number and book them in when they are returned. But people will be suspicious of numbered forms, so explain what the numbers are for and promise confidentiality and anonymity.

The Market Research Society (**www.mrs.org.uk**) has produced a very good code of conduct that provides useful guidance on issues of confidentiality.

The covering letter

This is crucial. A good covering letter can improve the response rate by ten or fifteen percentage points. What you have got to do is to motivate people to give you the information. Ask yourself what would motivate *you*? Self-interest, perhaps, or a desire to benefit others. So focus on what it is that the research is trying to achieve. Emphasize the importance of obtaining the views of people directly concerned. Stress the need to get as large a response as possible in order to take everybody's views into account.

Give people an indication of how long it will take them to complete the questionnaire; ideally this should be no more than ten minutes – longer than that and your response rate will suffer.

Tell them who you are doing the work for. People are more likely to respond to surveys carried out for government or voluntary sector bodies than they are to those for private companies – and market research companies are the worst of all. Give people an indication of what will happen to the results and, if possible, offer them an opportunity to receive a summary of the results.

If appropriate, promise anonymity or, failing that, promise that the results will be treated in the strictest confidence, that no individuals will be identified in the results and that the questionnaires will be destroyed after use.

Give people the name and telephone number of someone they can contact if they have queries about the survey.

Bear in mind that you need to get all of this on a single sheet of your headed notepaper.

Pre-tests and pilots

Once the questionnaire is distributed, you cannot get it back for correction. So you need to test it to ensure that it works. There are normally two stages of testing. First you pre-test by sending a draft of the questionnaire to one or two people who can be trusted to give you an honest opinion. This should include the client for the work and one or two other researchers who might be able to spot potential problems. Do not get despondent if you need to amend things at this stage. Remind yourself that time spent now will more than pay dividends later in the survey.

Then, having consulted the experts, try it with a few real people. Take a small group of respondents and send the revised version out to them under conditions that are as similar as possible to the real survey. See how they react and what difficulties they have in completing the forms. Again, be prepared to revise.

It is tempting to skip these two stages, particularly if the timescale is tight but there has never yet been a questionnaire that cannot be improved through pre-tests and a pilot. And there are few things more frustrating than dealing with a whole batch of questionnaires that have been completed wrongly because of a design error that you did not spot.

Response rates and reminders

On the covering letter and again at the end of the questionnaire you must give a date by which the questionnaires are to be returned. It is normal to give people two weeks to provide the information. Less than this can be thought unreasonable, but if you give people more they will forget about it.

Monitor the returned questionnaires as they come in, if possible, checking them off against your mailing list. You will get a surge towards the end of the first week and then it will tail off towards the closing date. Then you need to issue a reminder.

Reminders are most effective when they include a second copy of the questionnaire for those who have lost it. But this is expensive, so a simple letter is normally sufficient for a first reminder. If the response rate is still not very good three weeks after the closing date, send a second reminder. This time enclose another copy of the questionnaire and a new stamped addressed envelope.

The choice of a return envelope can be important. You can set up a reply-paid arrangement with the Post Office, but this usually takes a while. You will actually boost your response rate by four or five percentage points if you use an envelope with an actual stamp on it – people seem to feel guilty about wasting your money by not using the stamp.

If your requirement for anonymity is such that you cannot record who has sent their questionnaires back, you can still issue reminders but you have to do so to the whole sample, making it clear why everyone is being contacted again and apologizing to those who have already sent their forms in. You will probably get some who will send a second copy back to you but unfortunately you cannot avoid this.

E-mail surveys

For some groups, e-mail offers the best way of getting in touch. Most of the principles of questionnaire design apply – simplicity of language, and so on. But you will have to work hard to create a form that will transmit accurately to all respondents. If the form is embedded in the e-mail message it can easily be distorted in transmission and your nicely aligned boxes fly all over the place. You can, instead, put the form in an attachment but this is not without problems. Forms set up in one word-processing system will not necessarily appear so attractive if they have been converted to another.

You can overcome this to an extent by distributing the file containing the questionnaire in one of the common formats such as Rich Text Format, as an .rtf file. Or better as a .pdf file. People are more likely to get something that looks like the thing you sent them, although they may need special software like Adobe Acrobat in order to read it.

Currently response rates to e-mail surveys appear fairly good. This might simply be because they are novel. If so, make hay while the sun shines.

The two main problems are the selectivity of the sample. If you are surveying students or academics you can be fairly sure that they will all have e-mail addresses, but e-mail is still far from commonplace. The second problem is that it is almost certainly impossible to offer anonymity – all you can do is promise confidentiality.

Some people are beginning to mount surveys on websites. This can overcome some of the problems – like anonymity – and you can open up your survey to all-comers.

Web-based surveys of this kind are particularly useful when you are surveying use made of a website or when your sample population are known to be people who are at ease when using the Internet. It is a form of surveying that will undoubtedly grow in the years to come.

Interview surveys

Interview surveys have a great deal in common with self-completion surveys. The large-scale interviewing exercises like public opinion polls are really little more than questionnaires administered in person. They require a structured interview schedule which has many of the characteristics of a self-completion questionnaire. Semi-structured and depth interviews offer the interviewer more scope and these will be therefore dealt with in Chapter 14, 'Collecting Qualitative Data'.

In a structured interview, the interviewer reads out the questions and records the respondent's answers. The surveys are carried out like this for a number of reasons. First, it offers slightly more control over the response. In a quota sample, for example, the interviewer can press on until they have filled their quota. More particularly, the presence of an interviewer can reduce the number of refusals. It is more difficult to turn down a real person than it is to ignore a questionnaire.

Administered questionnaires can cover more complex topics, making far greater use of skips and filters than would be possible in a self-completion questionnaire. In some cases it is important to have questions asked in a particular sequence – an interviewer can do this, while a person filling in a self-completion questionnaire can read it through to the end before starting with question one. They can also be used to collect much more data – a good interviewer can conduct successful interviews that last up to 30 or 40 minutes, gathering a wealth of data in the process.

Face-to-face and telephone

Most interview surveys are conducted face-to-face. Interviewers visit people in their homes, stop them on the street or catch them when they are using a service. The personal contact can be used to persuade someone to take part in the survey and the ability to watch a person's body language can help the interviewer judge how best to get the information from the respondent.

Increasingly, however, people are being interviewed by telephone. This is much cheaper as it can be done from a call centre rather than having to send someone out and about. It does, however, have its problems. Many people are still not comfortable using the telephone – for this reason telephone interviews are more common when surveying businesses. Even some people who are at ease on the telephone feel that contact by an interviewer over the phone is an intrusion.

Prompts and probes

One of the main advantages of interviews is that the interviewer is able to explore people's responses in ways that are simply not possible with self-completion questionnaires. They can, for example ask a question and record the spontaneous response. They can then use a prompt to explore the response to a pre-determined list of choices. Supposing, for example, you wanted to explore the alternative ways of paying welfare benefits. You could ask someone how they would like to have their benefit paid, recording their spontaneous answer. You could then go on, using a show card, to draw their attention to the possible alternatives, asking them how they felt about those. This gets over the problem of people being unaware of the possibilities open to them or the fact that they have forgotten something.

A probe, on the other hand, is rather different. This is when the interviewer asks the respondent to provide a little more information or to explain the thinking that lies behind their response. A typical probe would be 'Can you tell me more about that?'

If you build prompts and probes into your structured interview schedule, you should be very careful to make it clear which questions are to be prompted and which to be probed.

Using professionals

Interviewing is a skill. It also requires a particularly robust personality – an interviewer has to be able to withstand rejection and to have the kind of personality that enables them to walk up to a complete stranger and, sometimes, ask them very personal questions. If you are planning to conduct an interview survey you would be well advised to subcontract the work to a fieldwork agency which will be able to help with the design and compilation of the interview schedule, will recruit the sample and will provide the interviewers. They will also normally process the results and provide you with tables.

In Chapter 2 we covered the steps that you need to take when subcontracting to research companies. Follow this advice and you could find that you have a very professional job that costs much less, and is done more quickly, than if you did it yourself.

One of the greatest advantages of using a fieldwork company is the fact that the interviewers will have been trained to ask the questions in a neutral and consistent way. This is not easily done and a novice interviewer can inadvertently introduce bias into an interview simply by reacting to the answers people give. If they respond differently to different people you could end up with data that are misleading.

One way in which fieldwork companies are able to offer a quick turnaround at a low price is through the use of CAPI and CATI. CAPI stands for Computer-Aided Personal Interviewing and CATI is Computer-Aided Telephone Interviewing. Instead of having the interview schedule on paper and writing the responses down, in CAPI and CATI surveys, the schedule is mounted on a computer and the interviewer records the responses directly onto the computer. At the end of the day, or the end of the shift, the completed responses can be transmitted directly to the main computer ready for analysis. This cuts out the cost of data input as well as the time involved. It explains how opinion poll companies can produce full results within a day or two of conducting a poll.

Postscript

Questionnaires and structured interviews are simply tools that enable you to collect data in standardized, easily analysed quantitative form. But they are tools that are susceptible to considerable refinement and sophistication. A blunt instrument will produce low-quality data. A well honed and refined instrument can gather data that is of very high quality and that fully justifies extensive analysis.

SUMMARY

The basic principle of sampling is simple: you take a sample of people and infer the characteristics of the whole group from those of the sample. It's from then on that things get more complicated.

The size of the sample is critical. The larger a sample, the more likely it is to represent the whole population. But the way in which the sample is selected is also important. Probability samples are selected on a random basis, sometimes stratifying the sample in order to produce respondents who are more conveniently grouped. Quota samples are less reliable statistically but make for cheaper surveys.

Self-completion questionnaires are the most common way of collecting quantitative data. They can use closed or open questions. Their design and layout are critical. They can determine the reliability of the responses. They can also have a big impact on the response rates.

Confidentiality and anonymity are important and it is worth adhering to a code of conduct produced by an organization like the Market Research Society. Questionnaires should be pre-tested and piloted to make sure they are free from errors. Use reminders to increase response rates.

E-mail and web-based surveys are becoming increasingly common, although they do have their drawbacks.

Interview surveys are similar to self-completion questionnaires. Many of the design features are common. They can, though, be used to collect more complex data, often using prompts and probes.

If you are contemplating an interview survey, think carefully about using a professional fieldwork company – they may well save you time and money and result in data that are more reliable.

13
Analysing quantitative data

You can now begin the task of converting data into information. Assuming that all has gone well with your survey you will have received back a large stack of questionnaires or completed interview schedules. What you now have to do is to process the data into a usable form, and to analyse it to produce the results from which you can begin to draw conclusions and so make recommendations.

Processing the data

Our ability to handle quantitative data has been transformed by computers. All the time we had to rely solely on manual processing we were limited in what we could do. Computers make it possible to carry out complex analysis quickly and relatively easily. If you are planning to make much use of quantitative data, therefore, you will almost certainly need to be thinking about using computer analysis.

Statistical analysis packages

There is a wide range of software that you can use to analyse quantitative data. You can, for example, do some fairly sophisticated analysis using standard spreadsheet software. This may well be the most appropriate choice for relatively small surveys that are going to be analysed in quite straightforward ways.

Then there are the packages specifically designed for data analysis. These come in different shapes and sizes, although the basic functions they perform are quite similar. Essentially they enable you to see not just how many people answered each question, but also how many of the people who answered 'yes' to question five, for example, also answered 'yes' to question ten.

The two market leaders are SPSS and Quantum, both now owned by the same company. SPSS, or the Statistical Package for the Social Sciences, is the standard within the academic community. It is now available in Windows format and is relatively straightforward to use. There are lots of training courses available and a number of user-friendly manuals. It is probably the most obvious choice for anyone entering the field.

Quantum is more commonly found in the market research world. It operates in a slightly different way from SPSS and many of its users claim that it is more sophisticated and capable of more complex analysis than SPSS. Unless you work in market research, however, it is less accessible. There are fewer copies available (like the full version of SPSS, it is very expensive to buy) and fewer training courses.

Before proceeding further you should select your analysis package because this will determine, among other things, the way in which your data will be entered.

Check and verify the returns

The first step in processing the data is to check and verify the returns as they come in. When you receive the completed questionnaires or interview schedules, go through them quickly. Make sure that all the questions have been answered and check to see if there are any obvious problems – lots of people crossing out and amending their answers to a particular question, for example.

You may not pick up many errors this way – you will surely find more later on – but you will get to know the data. You will begin the process of becoming familiar with the results. This is something that is difficult to describe but it is all about building up confidence in the data you are handling, becoming familiar with the coverage of the survey and the ranges of responses that people are making and generally starting to understand what it all adds up to.

Coding

If you have open questions you will need to code the responses. To do this, look at the responses to the first 20 or so returns that you receive. List all the responses that people have given to the open questions and then see if you can group them in any way. Ask yourself whether people are saying the same thing but in different words. For each question you should be able to classify the responses into five or ten broad categories. You can then use these categories to create a coding frame which you can use to code the responses on all the returns that follow.

If you are going to analyse the survey by computer, someone will need to input the data. This is known in the trade as 'punching the data', a term that was originally coined, like many others, in the early days when the main form of data entry was by using punched cards. To enable this to be done, each question will need to have a number or code and each response will also require its own code. You should have anticipated this when designing your questionnaires and the code number should have been printed on already. If not, slap yourself over the wrist and give the person responsible for the coding a blank questionnaire with the code numbers marked on it.

The task of actually inputting the data can be tedious and time-consuming. For most surveys of any size, it is normal to give the task to a specialist company. You give them the completed questionnaires and they give you back an electronic file containing the data. Clearly, if you are planning to subcontract the work in this way, it is a wise precaution to show a draft of the questionnaire to the company before you go into the field – they may well be able to make suggestions for design changes that will make their job easier – and the results consequently more reliable.

Cleaning the data

Before you go any further you must clean the data. What this means is that you must check it for errors and inconsistencies. The computer can perform some of these checks for you, others you have to do manually.

Basically what you are looking for is rogue data – things that are wrong or out of place. It may be that the questionnaire was completed incorrectly or there was a mistake in the punching. Your job now is to find those errors before they start distorting your results.

One thing you can do is to build in range checks. If, for example, you are asking about people's weekly income you can tell the computer to alert you to all the returns which have an answer outside the range £20–£1000 per week. Thus you will know if the inputter has keyed in 2000 by mistake when they should have entered 200.

You can also make logical checks – do you, for example, have many respondents under the age of five who claim to be married? Look at your basic frequencies. Are there any odd results? There will always be some outliers – respondents who for one reason or other fall outside the normal range – are they genuine or has there been a mistake? You usually have to go back to the original return and check it manually.

Only when you are sure that your data set is error-free should you begin to undertake the more complex analysis and interpretation.

Top-line data

The first output you will get will be what are known as frequencies or hole counts (again from the time when we used to punch holes in cards). This will tell you how many people gave each of the different answers to each question.

This will provide you with some useful information, particularly a breakdown of the types of people who responded to your survey. It will also tell you how many people were in favour of one thing compared to another. In an opinion poll, for example, it will tell you how many people intend to vote for each party. But you will probably need to go further.

Cross-tabulations

This is where the analysis packages come into their own. They enable you to produce cross-tabulations or, using the jargon, to undertake bivariate analysis. Taking the example of an opinion poll, you can easily see how many people would vote for each party, but you might also want to know how the voting intentions varied among different types of people. To do this you can set up a table with current voting intentions along one axis, then along the other axis you could provide a breakdown of respondents by sex, age, socio-economic class, age of completing education and so on. This would give you a much richer picture.

You might want to use this breakdown of respondents for other purposes – perhaps to see how people voted at the last election – in which case you would apply it in other tables. A breakdown used in this way is called a standard break, and it would be quite normal to produce an initial set of tables that analysed all the results by standard breaks.

Multivariate analysis

If you want to take things a stage further, you move into the field of multivariate analysis. This is the use of sophisticated statistical techniques to explore the extent to which individual variables affect each other. A wide range of variables can, for example, affect an individual's voting behaviour. These might include class, education, income, age, parents' voting behaviour, employment and so on. What multivariate analysis does is to look at each variable in turn to identify the strength of the causal relationship *other things being equal*. So, it would look at the strength of parental voting behaviour while holding all the other variables constant. In this way you can begin to develop a more detailed understanding of the underlying causes of something.

You can use SPSS to do a limited amount of multivariate analysis or modelling but if you want to exploit the potential to the full, you will probably need to use one of the specialist packages and to do that you will probably first have to find a tame statistician.

Interpreting the results

So, let us assume that you have checked and punched your data, you have cleaned it and have produced some basic frequencies or hole counts. You have then gone on to specify the basic cross-tabulations you want, using standard breaks and so on. You are now in a position to begin analysing and interpreting the results. Here, though, we must pause for a word on statistical significance.

Statistical significance

You will recall that in Chapter 12 we noted that the underlying principle of sampling was that you could look at the characteristics of a sample and from them infer the characteristics of the whole population. Your ability to do this depends on the size and randomness of the sample – in general, the larger and more random the sample the more statistically significant will be the results.

The statistical analysis packages will automatically calculate different tests of statistical significance. Table 13.1 provides an easy way of assessing whether or not your data are statistically significant.

Table 13.1 *Estimated confidence levels for a simple random sample*

Sample size	Percentage observed from the sample				
	10	20	30	40	50
50	8.3	11.1	12.7	13.6	13.9
100	5.9	7.8	9.0	9.6	9.8
250	3.7	5.0	5.7	6.1	6.2
500	2.6	3.5	4.0	4.3	4.4
1000	1.9	2.5	2.8	3.0	3.1
2000	1.3	1.8	2.0	2.1	2.2
3000	1.1	1.4	1.6	1.8	1.8
4000	0.9	1.2	1.4	1.5	1.5

What this table shows you is that if you have used a simple random sample of 250 people and have produced a result of 10 per cent you can be 95 per cent confident that the result will actually be 10 plus or minus 3.7 per cent or, in other words, the actual result will be between 6.3 and 13.7 per cent. In practical terms, this means that if your sample size is 250 and you find that 6.5 per cent of respondents prefer black but 12.5 per cent choose white, you cannot claim that white is more popular than black, *because the difference is not statistically significant.*

Incidentally, the table is symmetrical around 50 per cent, so for 60 per cent use the values in the 40 per cent column (60–100=40).

These figures are based on a simple random sample. If you use a quota sample, your variances increase. One leading market research company in Britain takes a cautious view and estimates that, for a quota sample, the table would look like Table 13.2.

Table 13.2   *Estimated confidence levels for a quota sample*

| Sample size | Percentage observed from the sample | | | | |
	10	20	30	40	50
50	12.8	17.1	19.5	20.9	21.3
100	8.9	11.9	13.6	14.6	14.9
250	5.6	7.5	8.6	9.2	9.3
500	4.0	5.3	6.0	6.5	6.6
1000	2.8	3.7	4.3	4.6	4.7
2000	2.0	2.6	3.0	3.2	3.3
3000	1.6	2.1	2.5	2.6	2.7
4000	1.4	1.9	2.1	2.3	2.3

These tables go to show how important it is to have large samples that are selected with a high degree of randomness. Unless you have large samples like this it is difficult to conclude that anything other than major differences are statistically significant.

So, armed with an understanding of the levels of statistical significance you can expect in your data, you can begin to try to make sense of it all. There are two main ways of approaching this. The first is an iterative approach that involves getting close to the data and developing your ideas as you go. The second is more structured.

Iterative analysis

If you adopt this approach you need to begin with a large set of tables – try to cross-tabulate everything with everything else. Then work steadily through all of the tables, looking to see what the data tell you. It need not be as random as it seems as you will begin with a basic set of expectations. You might expect, for example, that there would be no great difference in the voting intentions of men and women. But if you find that this is not the case then you have identified something that is interesting and possibly worth following up.

What you are looking for are exceptions and differences, patterns and trends. As your eye moves along the rows of the tables and down the columns, look for patterns and differences. If the figure in a cell is different from those around it, ask yourself why and see if you can find explanations in other tables.

As you work through the tables you will be building up an overall impression of things and getting a feel for what the data tell you. You can go back and double check, maybe running more tables to explore an issue in more detail. Keep circling around – iterating – until you feel you have understood all that the data can tell you, relating it all the time to the project's aim and objectives.

Structured analysis

If you think this is all a bit hit and miss, then you are probably more inclined to structured analysis. Here you begin with the aim and objectives of the project. You go back to your thinking when you designed the data collection tools, remembering what it was that you were looking for, what evidence you were trying to uncover.

From this you can build up an analytical framework that you can use as a basis for exploring the data. Rather than looking at everything to see what you can find, you will begin by running a few tables that are designed specifically to explore one of your key issues. The results of these may suggest other approaches or other tables you can run to produce information that you will need to confirm or refute the interpretations that are coming forward. You can then move on to the next issue and do exactly the same. As you work, new lines of enquiry may suggest themselves to you.

Again you will be looking for similarities and differences, for patterns and trends and for exceptions to those patterns. But you will be going further and asking yourself why things seem to be happening in the ways that they are, all the time looking for explanations and for ways of substantiating things.

SUMMARY

The first stage is to process the data so that it is ready for analysis. Before doing this, however, you need to decide which statistical package you will use for analysing the data. Very small surveys can be processed manually, slightly larger ones can be analysed effectively using spreadsheets, but for anything substantial you will need to use one of the statistical packages.

Check and verify the returns, looking for errors and odd results. Code the responses to open-ended questions so that the data is ready for inputting.

Once things have been punched, clean the data by again working through it, pulling out errors and inconsistencies. Where necessary, check back with the original returns.

139

You will then be able to produce the top-line data showing the frequency with which answers were given to each question. The next stage in sophistication is to produce cross-tabulations. To take things further means using multivariate analysis, which is technically sophisticated and usually requires the services of an expert.

When interpreting the results you must consider the statistical significance of your data. Broadly speaking, significance increases with the size and randomness of the sample.

You can adopt two basic approaches to analysing and interpreting the results. The iterative approach is more random and involves working your way through the tables and cross tabulations trying to spot differences and patterns. Or you can follow a more structured approach in which you pursue lines of enquiry that are suggested by the project's original aim and objectives.

14

Collecting qualitative data

Quantitative research aims to show you *what* is happening. Qualitative research, on the other hand, sets out to tell you *why* it is happening. It is all about developing a detailed understanding of individuals' views, attitudes and behaviour.

The approaches to collecting qualitative data are much less structured and formal than the techniques used for gathering quantitative data. The aim is to allow respondents to talk, often at great length, about their feelings, and about their underlying attitudes, beliefs and values.

Some qualitative research gathers data from individuals. Here, semi-structured and depth interviews are used to explore issues outside the tight constraints of a structured interview survey. Other techniques use groups of people to obtain a more considered picture, building on discussion and the development of individual views within a group setting.

Semi-structured interviews

For most people, the first step they take towards collecting qualitative data is through the use of semi-structured questionnaires. These can be thought of as a half-way house between the rigid formality of a structured interview – where the researcher attempts to fix and control the circumstances of the interview so that the data are collected in as consistent a fashion as possible – and the flexibility and responsiveness of a depth interview.

They are best used when you want to collect both structured information and information about attitudes or beliefs. This objective tends to determine the size of the sample to be used. The need to process some of the data in a quantitative way suggests that the smallest sample you can realistically contemplate is around 100 people. On the other hand, the need to make sense of the unstructured data will limit the sample to a maximum of about 200 people – more than that and you will end up analysing the qualitative data in a quantitative manner, so negating the purpose of the exercise.

You design the interview schedule in much the same sort of way as you would a structured schedule. Many of the questions will be closed, offering the respondent a limited range of options with the questions being asked in a pre-determined sequence. Other questions will be open-ended. The interviewer will be asked to record the answers verbatim, either writing the answer down or recording it on tape. You might list a number of prompts and probes that the interviewer can use to encourage the respondent, but what you are looking for is the respondents' spontaneous views.

Depth interviews

Depth interviews are very different. Here the aim is to range over a number of pre-determined issues but to do so in the way that best elicits the respondents' own views. Structured interviews call for an almost instant response on the part of the interviewee. Once they have answered a question the interviewer proceeds immediately to the next. There may be a little prompting and probing but it is all pretty spontaneous. Depth interviews, on the other hand, seek to explore *in depth* what it is that people feel about issues. Respondents are given time to think and to reflect on the questions that they are being asked – they are encouraged to elaborate and to explain in more detail the subtleties and complexities of their feelings.

Because the interviews explore issues in greater *depth*, it is seldom possible to cover the *breadth* of issues that you would in a structured or semi-structured interview. So you must be more selective in the issues that you cover, concentrating just on those that are most important.

Instead of starting with a questionnaire, or an interview schedule, the interviewer is given a topic guide that simply lists the issues that are to be explored, identifying any sub-issues or related concepts that need to be raised. The interviewers are then briefed about the background to the study, the nature of the research and the issues that are being explored.

Armed with the topic guide and the briefing, the interviewer establishes contact with the respondent, opening up a dialogue during the course of which they will cover all the points identified in the topic guide. The aim is to get respondents to talk in their own words and at their own level of understanding. The sequence in which the issues are raised is normally left open, allowing the interviewer to structure the conversation in the way that seems most appropriate. In some cases it may be necessary to cover some issues before moving on to others but the aim is to produce something that can be used as flexibly as possible.

It is possible just to make notes during a depth interview, but professionals always rely on some form of audio recording. We used to use tape recorders but digital recorders are now more common. One day it might even be possible to make a digital recording and then feed it through a natural language program to produce an instant transcript. We are still some way from that and it is still necessary to have the recording transcribed manually.

Depth interviews are used to collect data about attitudes, feelings, beliefs and behaviour from individuals. They provide a rich stream of data that can be used to build up an understanding of why things happen in the ways they do. Because the data collected is relatively unstructured, it is time-consuming to analyse. This, combined with the fact that the aim is not to collect data that is statistically representative, means that depth interview samples are normally quite small – 20 to 30 interviews would be normal.

Interviewing skills

Interviewing people in depth is a skilled task that is not to be undertaken by untrained researchers. The interviewers need to be able to overcome four main barriers that will impede the collection of reliable information. First, people will try to be more rational that you want them to be. You are trying to understand their emotions, views and beliefs, not what they think are the rational explanations for their behaviour. Related to this is the fact that most of us are unaware of our attitudes and beliefs – they are part of our subconscious – and it takes considerable skill to get people to articulate things that are not part of their daily thoughts. People also have a fear of being shown up. We each have our own self-image and we do not want this to be upset by what may be uncomfortable revelations. Finally, people will, in most cases, strive to be polite to interviewers and to supply the answers that they feel the interviewer is expecting.

To overcome these barriers you need to be as unobtrusive as possible, in every sense. You should dress in a way that will be acceptable and unsurprising to the people you interview. You should work hard to put people at their ease and to reassure them that their views are acceptable and entirely valid, but you need to do so in ways that do not encourage the interviewee to respond in a particular way. During the interview you should look at the respondent often enough to convey interest in what they are saying, but not so frequently that you appear to dominate or intrude.

Clearly, it is vital to reassure the interviewee that their remarks will be treated with absolute confidentiality and that no-one will be identified by name in the final report.

Throughout, you should encourage people to talk. Having put them at their ease, begin with concrete issues to which they can relate before moving on to discuss more abstract concepts. Keep the flow of information going with positive noises like 'hmm' or 'uh-uh'. If you want them to expand on something they have just said, do not ask a direct question that might steer them in a particular direction, instead say something like, 'That's interesting, can you tell me a little more about that?' Use silence – pause and look expectant and people will often take that as a cue to elaborate on what they have been saying. Alternatively, feed the information back to them by saying, 'You said that . . .' and then pause expectantly.

In general, approach issues directly, making the questions as straightforward and direct as possible, thus minimizing the risk of misunderstanding. If, however, you sense that a person is reluctant to tell you how they feel, approach the issue indirectly, ask them, 'How do other people around here feel about . . .?' If you need to judge strengths of opinion, then ask them to make comparisons between issues.

Try to ensure that you conduct the interview somewhere comfortable. Sitting in someone's living room will be more productive than standing on the doorstep. The interviews should be conducted one-to-one. Having another person present can severely constrain the flow of information. Try to look at things from the respondent's perspective. They will want to know what the research is all about – why they are being asked all these questions. They need to be reassured that the information will be used in confidence and that they will not be identified. And at the end of the interview they would like to be offered a chance to see what happens at the end of the day – the offer of a summary of the final report is usually very welcome.

Focus groups

These used to be called group discussions, which is a more accurate term. Now, however, market research companies use them a lot and the term focus group has become more common.

Depth interviews allow people to talk in detail about their beliefs and feelings. Focus groups force people to consider how they feel about issues in the light of other people's feelings. The essence is interaction between the members of the group, seeing how people moderate their views, react to different perspectives and manage their disagreements. They are discussions. What they should not become is a group interview where each member of the group is asked a set of questions, responding all the time to the interviewer. In a proper focus group, the interviewer chairs the discussion, steering it occasionally and ensuring that everyone has their say.

Only a small range topics can be covered in a focus group – three or four related issues is about the limit. One successful study, for example, used focus groups to explore just three issues – what health information people needed, what they received and what additional information they would have liked. The shortest discussion lasted one-and-a-half hours, the longest over three. So you really do need to focus down on the issues that are critically important. If you try to cover too much ground you will lose the depth and, with it, much of the potential offered by focus groups.

Clearly, the size and nature of the group is important. You should aim for between five and eight people. Fewer than five and it is difficult to get a sufficient range of views to make the discussion worthwhile; more than eight and the group is difficult to handle and some people will feel that they do not have sufficient opportunity to participate.

Some groups are selected from the general public. Here it is normal to use a market research company to recruit your groups for you. You specify the time and the type of group you are looking for – unemployed males over 40, for example – and the fieldwork company can arrange the rest. They can book suitable accommodation, arrange food and drinks – particularly important if it is an evening group – they can get the people there, using taxis if necessary, and get them home again afterwards and they can pay them the usual incentive fee. For that they will make a charge but, in nearly all cases, this is much less than it would cost in terms of your time if you did it yourself.

Alternatively, you can use an existing group – a tenants' association, perhaps, a social group, or one with a common interest in the subject which you are researching.

The advantage of the general public groups is that you get a wider spread of views but you have to work harder at getting them to coalesce as a group. The advantage of using existing groups is that they are easier to contact and you have a greater chance that they will have shared experiences. Against this is the fact that they will come with a pre-determined pecking order that you might have to counteract.

The time and place

Your aim is to ensure that the group covers the three or four topics that you have identified. To do this effectively you must ensure that everybody contributes and that all points of view receive a full airing. You should avoid conflicts and, above all, you should avoid steering the direction of the discussion.

Aim to hold the discussion somewhere that will be familiar and non-threatening to people. Someone's home is usually ideal, or a community facility such as a community centre or a meeting room in the public library. Rooms above pubs can be fine and are good for providing refreshments, but some people might object to them.

If you are using a market research company for recruitment, they may offer their own purpose-built facility. Some of these are very well equipped and can provide two-way mirrors so that others can observe the discussion, as well as video and tape recording.

Arrange the discussion for a time that will be convenient for the participants. This means evenings if people are working, or mid-morning if you want to get carers of school-age children. Avoid Fridays and Saturdays and check what is on the television – no point expecting men to turn out if there is an important football match on that evening.

Recording

You will need to record the discussion in some way. If you are responsible for the recording, make sure the recorder is working before you set out. If it is a tape recorder, check that you have enough new tapes. If it is digital, make sure you have enough memory. If it is mains-powered, take an extension lead in case there is not a conveniently placed socket. If it is battery-operated, make sure you have put new batteries in and that you have some more in reserve – just in case. When you arrive check everything again and make sure the recording level is acceptable. Then check it all for a third time just before the people arrive. Few things will upset the equilibrium of a discussion more than having you fiddle around with the recorder – you want people to forget about it as soon as possible.

Put people at their ease

When people arrive, put them at their ease. Tell them what the research is about and what you are hoping to discover as a result of the discussion. Make sure everyone is comfortable and, if appropriate, they have all got something to eat and drink. Try to arrange the chairs so that the members of the group are sitting in a fan-shape facing you. Make sure the people at the end are clearly visible to you or they will have difficulty catching your eye.

Explain that the discussion is being recorded, but reassure people that their remarks will be treated in confidence and that everything will be anonymized.

Ask each person to introduce themselves briefly, making it clear that no names will be used in the research – offer people the opportunity to use a pseudonym if they do not want to be identifiable on the recording (but be aware that most of them will forget their pseudonym within about five minutes). Have a note in front of you so that you can tell who is who in case you need to address them by name. If you need any other factual information about people ask them to fill in a brief questionnaire in advance – once they have arrived in the room the fewer things that hold up the discussion the better.

Encourage the group to chat to each other; this will enable you to size them up and, possibly, to identify those who will need to be encouraged and those who will try to dominate the discussion.

Chairing the discussion

Before people begin to get bored or to wonder when the whole thing is going to begin, start the discussion by making a simple statement, like, 'I would like to begin by discussing how you feel about . . .' Then pick on one of the quieter ones and ask them by name to say how they feel. Get the discussion going by asking who agrees or disagrees. This will enable the articulate ones to come in. But keep your eyes open for people who are a little reticent. Make sure that you bring them in as soon as possible – if someone has not spoken in the first ten minutes they will find it very difficult to break into the discussion.

If you feel the discussion is slipping off the point, bring it back by saying something like, 'Can we return to Mary's point about . . .? Does anyone disagree?' If someone is dominating the discussion, break into their flow by saying, 'That is very interesting. Mary, what do you think?'

If everyone seems to be in agreement, or if the discussion is going around in circles, introduce a new topic or move onto the next point. It is often helpful to summarize at this point, but keep it brief.

You will probably find that the discussion develops a momentum of its own and will require little intervention from you. Some useful questions to have in mind are:

> Some people have said . . . What is your view?
> I would like to ask some of the older/younger members of the group what they think about . . .
> Can I interrupt you there? I was interested in the point you made about . . . and I would like to see what other people thought about that.
> In another group people disagreed with that view. Does anyone here disagree?
> Earlier you said . . . What do you think about the point that Mary just made?

Keep your eye on the time. It is reasonable to expect people to give up about an hour and a half of their time – which will provide you with a full hour's discussion. Sometimes the group will clearly want to continue – you should be able to sense if they have still got a lot to say – in which case ask them if they want to break up or continue. Do not let it drag on beyond two hours. They will be getting tired; you will probably be exhausted by now. The tape recorder will be running out of tape and you will be facing a mountain of data to analyse.

Winding things up

Bring things to a close gently. People will almost certainly have asked you for your views. If not, they will certainly have been wondering. You should never express an opinion during the discussion – if asked you should say that it is important for you to keep an open mind, or that it is too soon to form an opinion – but at the end people often find it useful to have you tell them what you think, or what other groups have come up with. Then allow them a little time to disengage as a group. Do not bundle them all out of the door, let them drift off in their own time. This is particularly important if the discussion has in any way been emotional. Just chat about things in general – what a nice town they live in, what the sandwiches were like, what it is like doing research for a living, what you do in your day job.

Capturing the data

The problem that you have with qualitative data is that it comes in a free form that is not pre-determined. It is, therefore, difficult to set up mechanisms in advance to record the information in a neat, easily managed format. It is also difficult to be selective when you are capturing the data – at the time you do not necessarily know what will be important later.

Taking notes

The cheapest method is simply to take written notes during the interview or the focus group, perhaps supplementing these with fuller notes made immediately afterwards while things are still fresh in your mind.

The trouble with this is that you are forcing yourself to do too many things at once. You have to conduct the interview or the discussion, steering it in the right direction and exploring in greater depth the issues that are important. We have established that this is a skilled task that requires concentration. You need to listen to what is being said, analysing it as you go and separating the bits that are important from those that are not. You also have to write things down, getting the overall sense and recording verbatim the quotes that are going to be useful later on.

Clearly, it is difficult for any one person to do all this. Perhaps if you are fully versed in the subject and can tell instinctively what is important and if you can write very quickly, you might be able to get away with it. But, among other things, you will lose a lot of non-verbal clues as you will be looking at your notes rather than at the person you are interviewing.

If you do have to rely on notes alone, then check them immediately after the interview, expanding where necessary, rewriting things that are not clear and generally tidying things up. When you get back to the office, type up a full note of the interview, complete with quotations where you were able to record them.

Recordings and write-ups

The next step up in complexity is to record, on tape or digitally, the interview and to make notes yourself afterwards. During the interview you can concentrate on what is being said, relying on the tape recorder to capture it. You have much more control over the interview and a complete record that you can study in detail later. Do, however, make sure the recorder is working just before you start the interview and check immediately afterwards that you do, in fact, have a recording that you can understand. If not, panic and then start making notes as quickly as you can.

Try to listen to the recording and make notes as soon as possible after the interview – it will make less and less sense as time goes by. Listen to the whole recording first and then go back to the beginning. Take it in easily digested chunks. Listen to the tape, make sense of what is being said and note it down. Record verbatim any statements that encapsulate a theme or an idea so that you can use these later to illustrate points in the report. Do not be afraid to go back to listen again to points or to check inconsistencies or ambiguities.

Try to ensure that you have time, once you have taken your notes, to listen to the tape in full once more, checking and amending your notes as you go through.

Transcripts

The full works are when you record an interview or a discussion and then send the recording off to be transcribed. You will get back the full record that will probably run to many pages, a good few of which will contain nothing much of great interest. But you will have something that you can read, annotate and think about at your leisure. Furthermore, if you get an electronic version of the transcript, you can begin to contemplate using one of the computer-based systems for analysing qualitative data.

Transcribing tapes is a very skilled job – just try to read a transcript produced by someone who has never done it before. A good transcriber will take out all the 'ums' and 'ahs' and will marshal spoken words into sentences and paragraphs without, in any way, distorting the words the person actually used, but for that you should be prepared to pay. Ask around and find someone whom others can recommend, book the work in, remembering that good transcribers get booked up well in advance and make sure that you deliver the recordings when you say you will.

Make sure the recordings are of good quality. The person who sat through an interview will be able to make sense of a poor quality recording. But put yourself in the position of a transcriber. They probably know nothing about the subject and almost certainly will not know what any of the initials and acronyms mean. They will be coming to the voices for the first time and may have difficulty understanding accents. The recorder will have picked up all the background noises, muffling people's speech. They have to overcome all that to produce something that is meaningful. They also have to cope with the fact that while people may write in sentences they seldom speak in them.

SUMMARY

Qualitative research sets out to tell you *why* things happen. It aims to develop an in-depth understanding of individuals' views, attitudes and behaviour.

Semi-structured interviews come closest to quantitative data collection. Some questions are left open and the interviewer has to record the responses verbatim, sometimes prompting and probing to explore the issue in greater depth.

Depth interviews are completely unstructured. The interviewer has to rely on a general understanding of the issues to be researched and a topic guide that lists to specific issues to be covered in the interview. The aim then is to stimulate the respondent to talk about the issues in depth. This calls for considerable skill on the part of the interviewer who has to encourage the flow of information without steering or influencing the interview in any way.

Focus groups provide a means of exploring issues in even greater depth, allowing people to moderate their views in the light of those held by other members of the group. The essence is interaction and the group leader should do little more than ensure that everyone has their say and steer the discussion so that all the issues are covered.

Qualitative data should, ideally, be captured on a tape or digital recording, which can then be used to make notes or it can be transcribed to give a full verbatim record. Transcribing tapes is a skilled task and one that should not be undertaken lightly.

15
Analysing qualitative data

Many people think that, because you need to be able to work with computers and understand statistics, analysing quantitative data is harder than analysing qualitative data. After all, anyone can listen to a few recordings or read a dozen transcripts and make some kind of sense of them. They are wrong.

Analysing the results of qualitative research is a sophisticated and taxing process that calls for hard, concentrated effort, a clear mind and an intuitive approach to the data. If you are successful, the results can be impressive, leading to a deep understanding of issues and their causes. If unsuccessful, you can end up in an awful mess.

Basic principles of analysis

It is possible to identify some principles that underlie the analysis of qualitative data. Here I should acknowledge the work of Renata Tesch who in her book, *Qualitative Research: analysis types and software tools* (Routledge, The Falmer Press, 1990), has brought together a wide range of different approaches, most of them developed in the academic research community.

Analysis should not come last

Analysis should not just start when the data have been collected. You should begin thinking things through from the outset, trying to develop explanations and interpretations of the issues or circumstances that you are exploring. As the data are being collected you should be refining your ideas, questioning things and trying to see underlying reasons and causes. Analysis and collection should become integrated so that you can use what you deduce to inform in the next interviews or discussions.

Analysis should be systematic but not rigid

You should proceed in an orderly fashion with discipline. You should adopt an organized approach, pursuing lines of enquiry and documenting your work as you go on. You should only stop when new data no longer generates new insights. But throughout, you should strive to keep your mind open. Do not just look for evidence to confirm your early interpretations, look also for evidence to refute it.

Produce analytical notes as you go along

As you work through the data, pause every now and then and write a note to yourself setting down where you are and what you have concluded so far. These notes will help you to crystallize your thoughts and to track what you are doing and where you are going. They will also be invaluable if anyone else has to step in to help with, or take over the analysis.

Segment your data

Try to break the data up into meaningful fragments. These might be constructed around the issues you are exploring or around groups of people who have been interviewed. You cannot expect to hold all the data in your mind. These segments help you to process the data sequentially, thinking about chunks of it at a time. But you must not lose sight of the overall picture. Read through everything to begin with so that you will be able to relate your segments to the whole and keep trying to position the segments within the bigger picture.

Categorize the segments

You will need to impose some kind of order on the data. Try to arrange the segments systematically. Does this one relate closely to that one, or are they very different? Is this a subset of that? And so on. The categories themselves should be derived from the data and also, possibly, from the research objectives and your initial lines of enquiry. You should never have a segment that is not supported by the data.

Keep your categories flexible

Because your categories are derived from the data, they can never be fixed until you have exhausted the data. Some categories may become much bigger than others, possibly suggesting that they need to be subdivided. Something that starts by being self-evident may become more open to question as you sift through more evidence. Be prepared to revise and restructure. Remember that no order will fit the data perfectly.

The main intellectual tool is comparison

The main way you will impose order on the data is by comparing and contrasting. How does what this person said compare with that person's views? Is what this respondent said here consistent with what they said earlier in the interview?

There is no 'right' way to do things

Qualitative analysis is a very personal process and you must find the approach that suits you best. There are some basic rules and principles, there are also some mechanical techniques that will help you to manipulate the data, but in the end, you have to work through it trying to make sense of it all.

Intellectual craftsmanship

There are no rigid or mechanistic procedures. But you should not allow yourself to be limitlessly inventive. Find a way that works for you and apply it systematically and rigorously, refining it as you go.

Aim for a higher-level synthesis

You will begin by taking the data apart, breaking it up into segments and imposing an order on them. But your aim should be to achieve a synthesis that brings the segments together in new and original ways to throw light on the issues and to advance our understanding. The result of this higher-level synthesis should be a larger, consolidated picture that informs and enlightens.

The practice of analysis

So much for the principles. How can you best put them into practice? Well, we have seen that qualitative analysis depends greatly on personal preference. Some people like to listen to the recordings of interviews and group discussions, for example. Others prefer to read transcripts and to start from there. If you are doing it for the first time, you would probably be wise to do both – the closer you get to your data the better.

Identify themes and issues

Begin by working out what it is that you are looking for. You should be able to do this by referring back to the project's aim and objectives and to your topic guides. Identify the issues that you set out to explore in the research and the themes that informed those issues.

Read through a few of the transcripts or listen to some of the recordings and see if you have missed anything. Ask yourself whether, during the interviews or group discussions, anything struck you as significant or worth following up.

Then go back to your transcripts and recordings and, if you can, find the time to read through them all or listen to the recordings. What you are trying to do is to absorb the essence of those interviews and discussions. This is what qualitative research is all about – immersing yourself in the data so that you begin to understand what is going on in the respondents' minds.

Imposing order on the data

The next step is to impose some kind of order on the data. You can mark up the transcripts for all you are worth, annotating them to identify the points where they touch on your themes and issues. The difficult thing is to find a way of abstracting all those annotations and bringing everything together issue by issue, theme by theme.

Some people create a series of folders, one for each issue or theme. They then make extra copies of the transcripts and cut them up, putting each relevant segment in its folder. The problem with this is that you need to be able to relate the segment back to the person and so each needs to be coded in some way. Some people use numerical codes, others use colour coding, all according to preference.

You then have all the material grouped according to themes and issues. You can work through, folder by folder trying to understand what is going on, high-lighting quotes that illustrate particular points and shuffling the pieces of paper around until you get them into an order that seems to make sense. Some com-ments will naturally group together, others will clearly be different. You need to ask why this is. What type of people group together and who is separate? Do you find the same groups of people appearing over and over again, or is there no discernible pattern?

This approach is very flexible. It allows you to modify and adapt your cate-gories as the analysis proceeds and as new dimensions become apparent. The problem with it is, however, that it fails to give you a strong sense of who the people are. You need to keep referring back to your codes and it is difficult to build up a sense of the totality of a person – you have to work hard to relate an individual's response to one issue to their responses to all the others. And devel-oping an holistic approach of this kind is very important.

For this reason, some qualitative researchers prefer to use thematic grids to analyse their data. If you work best with pen and paper, get some big pieces of paper – at least A3 size, preferably bigger. The paper used in flipcharts is good. You then draw these up into grids with each cell being about eight or ten centimetres wide by five or six centimetres deep. Alternatively, do the analysis on your computer. Some people set up the grids on a spreadsheet, others use the tables facility in word processing software. Each row should represent a person and each column a theme or an issue.

Now you can work through each transcript and write into each cell the relevant material from the interviews. With group discussions, try if you can to identify the individuals and give each a row.

As you work through the material you will build up a good understanding of what is going on in the data. You will be able to see connections between different individuals' responses to particular issues and the ways in which particular individuals respond to different issues or themes.

It is not easy. It is time-consuming work and you need to be able to write in such a way that you get a lot of material into a small space without losing legibility. You also need to record where there are useful quotes, either on the grid or by referring back to the transcript.

Once you have transposed all the information you can pin the grids up on the wall, or spread them out over your desk and begin to make connections. Here a certain amount of doggedness is needed. You will find yourself going back over what by now will seem familiar ground and then going over it all again. What you are looking for are things that will confirm or refute your initial assumptions. You are looking for evidence that will throw light on the issues, but more than that, you are trying all the time to relate that evidence back to the circumstances of the individuals. Why did she say that? It contradicts what she said about this. What is the explanation? Was there a reason why this person said one thing and that person said something different when on other issues they are in agreement?

You need to keep working at the data until you feel that it is not giving you any new insights. The trick is to exhaust the data before it exhausts you.

It is not something that can be done easily or quickly. But what it does is to give you a very thorough understanding of the subject and the way people feel about it.

Computer packages

There are computer packages that you can use for the analysis of qualitative data. The two best known are NUDIST and Ethnograph. Essentially they use the computer's capacity to search and find specified terms in much the same way that word-processing systems can.

To use the packages you first have to have your transcripts in machine-readable form. You then go through them adding in or highlighting key words and key concepts. The packages then allow you to search for these terms and retrieve the relevant sections of the transcripts. The basic principle is much the same as the manual approaches using folders or grids.

Some people find these packages very useful; often they are people who have done a lot of computer-based analysis of quantitative data. People who come from a qualitative background sometimes feel, on the other hand, that the packages fail to give them the intimate familiarity with the data that is so important in qualitative research.

Descriptive or analytical

Some qualitative research merely describes what is going on. In its place, this may be useful and it is a necessary first stage in the process of making sense of the data. What you should aim to do, though, is to take things further and develop an analytical approach. You should move from asking *what* is going on and begin to ask *why* it is happening.

To do this, try to predict what people will do under certain circumstances – ask yourself what you would do. From this build tentative models or explanations of behaviour and then test them against the data you have. Do other people behave in the way you would under the circumstances? If they do not, why not? Have people responded or reacted in the way you would expect? What does the evidence tell you? Try to work out why people respond in different ways, look for explanations in their circumstances and backgrounds.

Remember that qualitative research is different from quantitative. Quantitative data is very good for telling you *what* is happening. Qualitative provides an insight into the deeper question of *why*?

SUMMARY

Analysing the results of qualitative research is a sophisticated and taxing process that calls for hard, concentrated effort, a clear mind and an intuitive approach to the data.

There are certain basic principles that should guide your analysis of qualitative data:

- Analysis should be thought about early in the research
- Analysis should be systematic but not rigid
- Produce analytical notes as you go along
- Segment your data
- Categorize the segments
- Keep your categories flexible
- The main intellectual tool is comparison
- There is no 'right' way to do things
- Practise intellectual craftsmanship
- Aim for a higher-level synthesis.

Putting these principles into practice means first of all identifying themes and issues, and then referring back to the project aim and objectives and to your experience of the fieldwork.

Then impose some order on your data. Some people choose to use folders to group relevant information together. Others find thematic grids more satisfactory. Computer packages are available, but they have received a mixed reception among the qualitative research community.

Work through the data looking for explanations. Your aim should be to move from description to analysis.

16
Sources of further reading

Bell, Judith (2005) *Doing Your Research Project – a guide for the first time researcher in education, health and the social sciences*, 4th edn, Open University Press.

Aimed at students, the book covers much the same ground as this one does. I shall leave you to judge which does it better.

Bernard, H Russell (2000) *Social Research Methods: qualitative and quantitative approaches*, Sage.

All you ever wanted to know - and more.

Black, Thomas (1999) *Doing Quantitative Research in the Social Sciences: an integrated approach to research design, measurement and statistics*, Sage.

A good introductory text that aims to cover the whole research process. It is aimed more at students than at practitioners.

Blalock, Hubert M (1979) *Social Statistics*, 2nd edn, McGraw-Hill.

All you ever wanted to know about statistics but were afraid to ask. First published in 1960 and revised in 1979, this is still a key text for people interested in the statistical side of social research.

Bryman, A (2004) *Social Research Methods*, 2nd edn, Oxford University Press.

A very thorough, well thought-of basic guide to research. It is aimed mainly at students but there is much here for practitioners. There is a companion website.

Creswell, J (2003) *Research Design: qualitative and quantitative approaches*, 2nd edn, Sage,

Aimed mainly at students.

Cutts, Martin (2004) *The Oxford Guide to Plain English*, Oxford University Press.

An excellent book by Britain's foremost exponent of plain writing. There is much practical guidance here for people producing questionnaires and for those who want to write reports that people can understand.

De Vaus, D A (2001) *Surveys in Social Research*, 5th edn, Routledge.

This is rather academic in tone, but it provides a very full and authoritative guide to the subject.

Fink, Arlene and Kosecoff, Jacqueline (1998) *How to Conduct Surveys: a step-by-step guide*, 2nd edn, Sage.
A very practical guide to survey design and conduct.

Foster, Jeremy (2000) *Data Analysis for Using SPSS for Windows Version 8.0–10.0: a beginner's guide*, Sage.
A down-to-earth guide to the most popular statistical analysis package.

Gilbert, Nigel (ed) (2001) *Researching Social Life*, Sage.
An excellent collection of introductory papers out of the stable at Surrey University that produces *Social Research Update*. It is both authoritative and practical.

Gorman, G E and Clayton, Peter (2004) *Qualitative Research for the Information Professional: a practical handbook*, 2nd edn, Facet Publishing.
Although aimed at information professionals, this is a very thorough guide to qualitative research that would be accessible by anyone interested in its application in organizational research.

Gray, David E (2004) *Doing Research in the Real World*, Sage.
This mainly deals with research methods but does so in an accessible way.

Hart, Chris (1998) *Doing a Literature Review*, Sage; and (2001) *Doing a Literature Search*, Sage
Both these books may be a little basic for the skilled information professional. But if your skills are a little rusty . . .

Healey, J F (2002) *Statistics: a tool for social scientists*, 6th edn, Wadsworth.
Another good guide to statistics and their use, although some may find it a little heavy going.

Jowell, Roger, Thomas, Roger and Lynn, Peter (2006) *Survey Research Practice*, Sage.
This originated as Gerald Hoinville's 1978 publication, which was considered by many to have been a classic. Revised and updated by three of Britain's leading professional survey researchers, it is very authoritative and full of sound practical advice and guidance.

May, Tim (2001) *Social Research: issues, methods and process*, 3rd edn, Open University Press.
Tim May successfully bridges the gap between theory and methods in social research. The book is divided into two parts. Part I examines the issues and perspectives in social research and Part II sets out the methods and processes.

Miller, Robert and others (2002) *SPSS for Social Scientists*, Palgrave Macmillan.
This book provides the novice user with a step-by-step guide to SPSS – easily the most widely used data analysis computer package in the social sciences. Written in a clear and non-technical style, the book takes a

practical and task-oriented approach to social science data analysis, building up understanding and confidence on the part of the reader in a carefully constructed and supportive way.

Moser, C and Kalton, G (1985) *Survey Methods in Social Investigation*, Dartmouth.

A key text that has stood the test of time. It is a very thorough, if a little dated, guide to social surveys. It is currently out of print but worth finding in the library.

Orna, Elizabeth and Stevens, Graham (1995) *Managing Information for Research*, Open University Press.

A practical guide to keeping your information straight. No more boxes of papers tucked away under the desk. The book covers more than just organizing your data, it provides an information perspective on the whole research process.

Punch, Keith (2005) *Introduction to Social Research: quantitative and qualitative approaches*, 2nd edn, Sage.

Another good introductory text aimed at both students and practitioners.

Ritchie, Jane and Lewis, Jane (eds) (2003) *Qualitative Research Practice: a guide for social science students and researchers*, Sage.

The authors work for the National Centre for Social Research and, therefore, do qualitative research for a living. The book covers the entire process of qualitative research from beginning to end – moving through design, sampling, data collection, analysis and reporting.

Saratakos, D (2005) *Social Research*, 3rd edn, Palgrave Macmillan.

Very thorough but rather heavy going.

Silverman, David (2005) *Doing Qualitative Research*, 2nd edn, Sage.

Aimed at students but packed with useful information for research practitioners of all kinds.

Social Research Association (2005) *Commissioning Social Research: a good practice guide*.

A practical guide to all the things you need to think about when commissioning research. Useful in two ways: it tells you what sponsors will be looking for when commissioning you to do research for them, and it tells you what to think about when you are subcontracting to others. Available from the Social Research Association at admin@the-sra.org.uk or from their website: www.the-sra.org.uk/documents/pdfs/commissioning.pdf.

Social Research Update, Department of Sociology, University of Surrey.

These updates are useful, compact packages of information and give practical advice on an eclectic range of social research issues. They are produced by people with practical expertise and, while the quality is variable, they are building up into a valuable resource for social researchers.

Social Research Update is available from the Department of Sociology, University of Surrey, Guildford GU2 5XH, England. Subscriptions for the hardcopy version are free to researchers with addresses in the UK. Apply to SRU subscriptions at the address above, or e-mail sru@soc.surrey.ac.uk. The updates are also available on the University of Surrey website: www.soc.surrey.ac.uk/sru/sru.htm.

The Survey Methods Unit Newsletter, Survey Methods Unit, National Centre for Social Research.

A regular newsletter, now in e-mail form, that discusses practical social research issues. Worth subscribing to if you have more than a passing interest in social research.

Further details are available at: www.natcen.ac.uk/natcen/pages/nm_newsletters. htm#smunews.

Tesch, Renata (1990) *Qualitative Research: analysis types and software tools*, Routledge, The Falmer Press.

Do not be put off by the rather academic feel of this book. It contains a great deal of very useful information and practical advice on the analysis of qualitative research results.

Trustfunding.org.uk

An authoritatiove website that provides information on over 4200 grant-making trusts with a total of over £3.1 billion a year to dispense. It is, therefore, an invaluable resource for people wanting to finance their research. Available on subscription at: www.trustfunding. org.uk/Default.aspx.

Wright, Daniel (1996) *Understanding Statistics: an introduction for the social sciences*, Sage.

Those who find Blalock a little heavy-going might try this one. It is rather more practical and is aimed at making statistics comprehensible for social scientists.

Appendix

The market for information professionals
A proposal from the Policy Studies Institute

> Libraries are undergoing a series of transformations, and the total effect of these changes amounts to a revolution in the way we deliver our services, our whole philosophy of service and how we are organised (Corrall, 1995)

Nowhere are the consequences of these transformations felt more strongly than in the employment market for information professionals. Changes in the culture of information use; in the expectations and practices of users and in the technology of information handling all have an impact on the employment market for information professionals.

Employers are seeking new combinations of skills. Practitioners are confronted with rapidly shifting job requirements. In such circumstances, competencies may become more valuable than qualifications, while professional accreditation is likely to carry less weight than once it did.

Topical though these issues are, they are not new. The employment market for information professionals has been in the process of long-term change for the last thirty years.

During the early 1970s the main pre-occupation was with balancing the supply of and the demand for librarians and information workers (Library Association, 1977). Later in the decade, attention shifted towards new skill requirements as it began to become apparent that the growth in the amount of information available was changing the nature of the demands placed on librarians and information workers. In such circumstances, information professionals were becoming less able to exercise the fairly erudite set of craft skills which they had developed over the previous thirty years (Moore, 1986b; Debons and others, 1981).

During the 1980s the demand for information professionals changed significantly. Many new jobs were created and many of them called for a different range of skills. It was possible to see a greater requirement to possess basic information technology skills (Oppenheim, 1983; Angell, 1987). It was also possible to identify the emergence of a new class of information professionals – researchers and information analysts (Moore, 1987 and 1988). The changes were happening in Britain and in other information-intensive countries like Singapore (Moore, 1986a), Australia (Broadbent, 1984; Lane, 1982) and the USA (Koenig and Kochoff, 1984). During this period questions were frequently raised about the ability of the education system to produce new professionals with appropriate skills and abilities (Cronin 1983b).

Ten years on it is clear that the situation has continued to change radically. Much of the change is attributed to technological development (Bauwens, 1994). This has produced changes in the patterns of information behaviour among users. Put simply, more and more people are using information in their work and at home. There is also more information around and it is more highly processed than ever before. This certainly applies to electronic information but we should also remember that there has been a comparable (and continuing) explosion in the amount of printed information published – the number of titles published each year in Britain grew by 50 per cent between 1990 and 1995 while the number of books sold grew by 20 per cent (Cultural Trends, 1997). User-friendly systems enable users to retrieve the information they need. And there is an expanding information industry promoting a culture of intensive information use.

Information is becoming embedded in our culture, shaping the way in which we work, play and enrich ourselves. In such circumstances, some people argue that there is little need for information professionals as everyone is becoming more professional in their use of information (Abell, 1996). The counter-view is that the heightened awareness of, and demand for information will stimulate a corresponding rise in the demand for information professionals (Infield, 1996). The question then becomes, what skills and abilities will be required by those professionals, and how will they differ from what we have known before?

The purpose of this proposed study is to explore the nature and extent to which the skills required by information professionals have changed over the last ten years, using the research that the British Library funded in the mid-1980s as a baseline. We propose also to look at the qualifications, skills and experience offered by individuals appointed to jobs as information professionals. From this it should be possible to identify the range of skills that are likely to be required in the future.

The study will complement other work taking place in the information skills area such as the Skills for new information professionals project in Plymouth (Garrod, 1996) and the Educational Development for Higher Education Library Staff. These projects are concerned with the skills required by information professionals but within the context of a single employment category. We will be looking across the board and will thus provide a context within which the results of other studies can be considered.

Aim and objectives

The aim of the study is to identify the range of skills that will be required by future information professionals. We will do this by exploring the range of skills, qualifications and experience required by employers of information professionals in the late 1990s; assessing the extent to which these requirements have changed over the last ten years and comparing the requirements with the characteristics of people applying for such positions. Within this overall aim, therefore, the study has three specific objectives:

- To analyse the range and nature of the skills required by employers who are actively recruiting information professionals and to identify the extent to which employers are able to satisfy their requirements.
- To assess the extent to which people recruited to jobs as information professionals meet the employers' requirements and from this to assess the relevance of education and training provision.
- To explore with both employers and employees the ways in which skill requirements are likely to develop in the future.

Methods

The British Library-funded research into the skill requirements of information professionals in the mid-1980s (Moore, 1987) used a novel, but highly effective technique to survey current skill requirements. The technique used job advertisements to identify the population of relevant jobs currently on offer. Having identified the population it becomes possible to survey the employers to identify their perceptions and requirements both before and after the actual selection of an employee. It is also possible to survey the employees themselves after they have taken up their new positions.

Employers are highly motivated to respond to the surveys as they have a significant stake in the recruitment of suitable individuals and are keen to pick up any possible intelligence about the employment market. Newly-appointed employees are also highly motivated, for much the same reasons. The surveys, therefore, achieve high rates of response – we confidently expect to achieve response rates in excess of 60 per cent.

Such surveys also collect information that represents the most up-to-date thinking by employers as well as the realities of the employment market at the time of the research.

We propose to use this technique again, scanning all relevant publications over a twelve-month period to identify the overall picture of recruitment. The 1985 survey focused on jobs in the 'emerging' market and identified 1106 posts advertised between June 1984 and May 1985. We feel certain that the overall level of demand has risen considerably since then and we expect to identify closer to 1500 advertised posts. Assuming a project start in October 1997, we would scan job advertisements published between February 1997 and January 1998.

Clearly, it will be important to define quite precisely what we mean by an information professional. The original British Library project identified 10 categories of information professional (Moore, 1987). In subsequent studies (Moore, 1986a and 1988) it was possible to consolidate some of these categories into three broad types:

- *Librarians and information workers*: professionals who are concerned with establishing, maintaining and exploiting a collection in expectation of future use.
- *Researchers and information analysts*: professionals who draw on a range of information sources to assemble information in response to specific enquiries then, having gathered the information together, analyse, digest and re-package the information for use by the enquirer.
- *Information systems specialists*: professionals who are concerned with the information management issues associated with information technology systems. They frequently act as the interface between the users and the IT specialists and their task is to add value by converting data into information and making the products accessible for use by others. They are often required to develop an organisation's information systems strategy.

The last of these categories proved to be very difficult to define satisfactorily and the studies ended up collecting a considerable amount of information that properly related to computer professionals. The boundaries between a specialism in the technology and in the information were blurred in the mid-1980s and have since become even more indistinct. Many computing courses, for example, now focus on information management issues. We, therefore, propose to focus on the first two categories of information professional where the emphasis is clearly on the handling of information as distinct from the operation of information technology.

Having obtained the overall picture we will focus on the jobs advertised in the last three months – November 1997 to January 1998 – and survey all employers advertising relevant positions during that period. This should give us a sample size of about 350 posts and, probably, 300 employers. We will contact them at the point when the post is advertised and again three months later when it is likely that the post will have been filled. We will seek to discover what expectations the employer had and the extent to which they were realised.

All employers will be contacted by post. To provide more detailed information we will survey a sample in-depth by telephone.

Five months after the post was first advertised we will survey the newly-recruited employees, again using a postal survey complemented by in-depth telephone interviews. This survey will take place during the period from June to August 1998.

We will also need to take account of the recruitment agencies which specialise in the information sector. Such agencies were relatively rare at the time of the 1985 survey but now they are much more common. We will conduct in-depth, face-to-face interviews with senior executives in each of the specialist recruitment agencies and will seek their agreement to include posts they advertise in the two samples of the main survey.

It will be extremely useful to organise a small number of events to discuss and consider the results of the research with different constituencies. We propose to organise three round-table discussions with samples of employers, with the directors of the specialist recruitment agencies and with heads of courses at relevant education and training institutions. For each discussion we will produce a background briefing paper, setting out the preliminary results of the research and identifying trends and significant issues. We will ask each discussion group first to comment on and to validate the results and then to consider the likely future developments.

These round-table discussion meetings will be an integral part of the research – they will provide a valuable opportunity to discuss the preliminary findings with informed audiences. They will also, however, provide an early opportunity to disseminate the results of the research.

The final results will be made available in an accessible report. The Policy Studies Institute has an active publishing and dissemination programme and would welcome the opportunity to publish a book containing the research results. PSI places a very high priority on the active dissemination of results and we would, therefore, wish to hold a conference to promote awareness of the results and to use them to stimulate wider discussion on the issue. It would also be possible to organise such a conference or seminar at PSI but this has not been allowed for in the costing.

Timescale

The duration of the study will be from October 1997 to September 1998. During this period the different tasks will be undertaken as follows:

- Scanning overall sample of advertisements: November 1997–January 1998
- Detailed survey of three months of advertisements: December–January 1998
- Survey of recruitment agencies: February–April 1998
- Survey of employees: May–July 1998
- Analysis: April–May 1998 and July–August 1998
- Round table discussions: July–August 1998
- Report: September 1998.

The Policy Studies Institute

PSI is Britain's leading independent research organisation, undertaking studies of economic, industrial and social policy and the workings of political institutions. PSI is a registered charity, run on a non-profit basis, and is not associated with any political party, pressure group or commercial interest. In 1989 the Institute established its Information Policy Group (now re-designated as the Culture and Communication Group) which has since undertaken a wide range of studies in Britain and for the European Commission.

Project staff

The project will be carried out within the Culture and Communication Group by Nick Moore and Adrienne Muir.

Nick Moore is the Head of PSI's Culture and Communication Group. He has over twenty years of experience of research and consultancy gained in Britain and overseas. His main areas of interest are the information workforce and the development of information policy. He has just completed a two-year secondment to the British Council where he studied the development of information societies in East Asia. Before joining PSI he was Professor of Information Management at Birmingham Polytechnic.

Nick Moore will be responsible for the overall management and direction of the project.

Adrienne Muir is a Research Fellow in the Culture and Communication Group. She has considerable experience of policy-orientated research gained through her two years at the Policy Studies Institute. During this time she has contributed to a number of studies within the Group and through this has gained experience of work within a European context. She has also made a significant contribution to PSI's quarterly analytical publication *Cultural Trends*. She has a Master's degree from Strathclyde University. Before joining the Institute she worked for the National Library of Scotland.

Adrienne Muir will undertake the bulk of the research. She will be responsible for all the surveying, including the depth interviews with key informants.

Costs

The total costs of the study are:

- Staff costs   £24,500
- Travel and subsistence   £ 2,400
- Recurrent costs   £ 2,600
- Other costs   £   450
- Total   £29,950

A full breakdown of costs is given on the enclosed application form.

References

Abell, A (1996) The Information Professional in 1996, *Information Management Report*, (January), 1–6.

Angell, C (1987) *Information, New Technology and Manpower*, British Library.

Aslib (1996) *The Future Information Professional: proceedings of a conference organised by Aslib, May 1996*, Aslib.

Bauwens, M (1994) Cyberspace, Virtualization and the Role of Cybrarians, *FID News Bulletin*, **44** (7/8), 131–7.

Broadbent, M (1984) Information Management and Educational Pluralism, *Education for Information*, **2** (3), (September), 209–27.

Corrall, S (1995) Information Specialists of the Future. In *Information Superhighway: the role of librarians, information scientists and intermediaries*, Universitätsbibliotek Essen.

Cronin, B (1983a) *The Education of Library/Information Professionals: a conflict of objectives*, Aslib.

Cronin, B (1983b) *The Transition Years: new initiatives in the education of professional information workers*, Aslib.

Cultural Trends (1997) *Books, Libraries and Reading*, No 26, Policy Studies Institute.

Debons, A and others (1981) *The Information Professional: a survey of an emerging field*, Dekker.

Garrod, P (1996) Skills for the New Professional, *Library Technology*, 1 (5), 1996, 99–100.

Infield, N (1996) Dealing with Disintermediators, *Library Manager*, 18, (May).

Koenig, M and Kochoff, S (1984) The Emerging Role for the Librarian in Data Administration, *Special Libraries*, 75 (3), (July), 238–46.

Lane, N (1983) Librarianship: a profession in context. In *The Library Workforce: Proceedings of a National Conference, Melbourne, 1982*, Library Association of Australia, 128–57.

Library Association (1977) *Report of the Commission on the Supply of and the Demand for Qualified Librarians*.

Moore, N (1986a) *Guidelines for Information Workforce Surveys*, Unesco.

Moore, N (1986b) *The Library and Information Workforce: a study of supply and demand*, Parker Moore.

Moore, N (1986c) *Adding Value to Information: the role of information professionals*, Singapore Library Association.

Moore, N (1987) *The Emerging Market for Librarians and information specialists*, British Library.

Moore, N (1988) *Information-intensive Management: its impact on the employment market for information professionals*, Aslib.

Moore, N (1996) Creators, Communicators and Consolidators: the new information professionals, *Managing Information*, (June), 3 (6), 24–6.

Oppenheim, C (1983) The Impact of Information Technology on Information Science: implications for courses in the UK, *Education for Information*, 1 (2), (June), 125–37.

Index